UNDERSTANDING THE HUMAN FORM

a practical study & workbook for human surface anatomy

Frank D. Shapiro, Chairman
Department of Fine Arts
Fashion Institute of Technology

Arnold Burchess, Former Chairman
Department of Fine Arts
Fashion Institute of Technology

Harriet E. Phillips
Medical Illustrator

AVERY PUBLISHING GROUP INC.
Wayne, New Jersey

Contents

Preface

This is the first workbook approach to the study of the human body. Designed to instruct the student of anatomy, it first provides clear, plainly labeled anatomical plates, each of which is accompanied by explanatory text. This Study section is followed by a Work section containing a series of fill-in plates; every plate corresponds to a plate in the first section of the book. Work Plates are removable and may be submitted to instructors when and if they so desire.

No one text can adequately explain or depict how a muscle or group of muscles look in the various poses and actions of the human form. That should be the instructor's task. This book is an *aid* to instructors, providing students with a handy reference and a reinforcement of visual memory.

At the Fashion Institute of Technology, we discovered that having students work on plates of predrawn and standardized skeletons, etc., greatly simplified not only their work, but also the work of the instructors. Work became uniform, easy for students to draw, and easy for instructors to check.

This approach, in fact, worked out so well that we felt it should be enlarged to include the actual anatomical plates. We have done so in a format that enables students to keep their completed workbook as a handy reference. The work included may, obviously, be assigned to more than one semester, used in conjunction with life drawing classes (as we do at FIT), or used in separate anatomy classes.

This book is strictly an analysis of skeletal and surface muscular anatomy; no attempt is made to teach the student to "draw" the figure. The text begins with a section on the skeleton of the body, head, neck, hands, and feet. Following this is a series of plates on the muscles of the torso, arms, legs, head, neck, hands, and feet. The muscles are clearly shown in red on top of the skeletal drawings, and the origin, insertion, and action of the muscles are included on the bottom or reverse side of each page. We have attempted to show all surface muscles or sub-surface muscles which influence the surface form on *individual* plates, and in all the main views in which they may appear: front, back, side, or outside and inside. This procedure enables the students to find all the information regarding a particular structure on the same plate, instead of having to search through the entire volume.

In cases where the muscles are too minor to have a full page devoted to them, textual material concerning them will be found on one of the assembled arm, leg, or torso views. In order to keep the length of the book reasonable, the head, hand, and foot muscles are found only in the assembled views.

This text, in addition, includes plates illustrating fatty tissue distribution, the differences between the male and female skeletons, and other important anatomical features. For most plates, there are corresponding Work Plates for the student to complete.

Understanding the Human Form is an enormous aid to both teachers and students, beautifully complementing the classroom use of a skeleton or model, and supplying students with a concrete method of testing their understanding and retention of the subject matter.

Introduction

Since the beginning of the Renaissance, the study of anatomy has been regarded as a necessity for an artist. As the arts of the West were fundamentally figurative, it was important for painters and sculptors to master the field of human anatomy at least that of surface anatomy. The work of Renaissance painters such as Ghirlandaio and Signorelli, and sculptors such as Verrochio and Donatello shows their knowledge of anatomy. The great masters such as Leonardo da Vinci and Michelangelo not only studied anatomy, but also dissected the human body; Leonardo's anatomical drawings are famous. Later, Mannerist artists and Baroque artists such as Bernini had a remarkable knowledge of human surface anatomy.

The artists of other countries and centuries were equally well versed in the field. Rembrandt painted the *Anatomy Lesson*. The great American painter Thomas Eakins was, for a time, a professor of anatomy.

In the last fifty years, the study of anatomy has increasingly been disregarded as part of an artist's background. The recent renewal of interest in "realism" and figurative painting and sculpture, however, has made many art students desirous of such training, and art schools have enlarged their offerings in such study. Artists have once more realized that no one can possibly handle the various problems involved in the representation of the human form in a realistic fashion, without understanding human anatomical structure. While it is true that such knowledge will not transform people into artists, lack of such knowledge will be a perpetual drag on an artist's ability to do creative work. The matter may be considered analagous to the problems of an engineer who is trying to function without a knowledge of mathematics.

This book was designed to simplify your mastery of human anatomy. Its unique workbook approach provides you with both the essential information regarding the surface structures of the human body, and a means of testing your understanding and retention of this information .

Understanding the Human Form is divided into two main sections: The Study Book and the Work Book. The first part of the book ––the Study section–– provides clear, plainly labelled anatomical plates, each of which is accompanied by explanatory text. The work section of the book contains a series of corresponding fill-in plates. After studying the plates in the first section, you will complete the drawings and notes in the second section.

Topic coverage begins with a section on the skeleton of the body, head, neck, hands, and feet. Following this is a series of plates on the muscles of the torso, arms, legs, head, neck, hands, and feet. The muscles are clearly shown in red on top of the skeletal drawings, and the origin, insertion, and action of the muscles are included on the bottom or reverse side of each plate. We have attempted to show all surface muscles or sub-surface muscles which influence the surface form on *individual* plates, and in all the main view in which they may appear: front, back, side, or outside and inside. This format will enable you to find all the information regarding a particular muscle on one plate, instead of having to search through the entire volume.

In cases where the muscles are too minor to have a full page devoted to them, textual material concerning them will be found on one of the assembled arm, leg or torso views. The head, hand, and foot muscles are found only in the assembled views.

The book, in addition, includes plates illustrating fatty tissue distribution, the differences between the male and female skeletons, and other important elements of anatomy. For most plates, there are corresponding Work plates for you to complete.

Conscientious study and use of this text will help you to understand how surface anatomical structures determine the unique form of each individual, and to apply this knowledge to the successful rendering of the human body.

STUDYBOOK

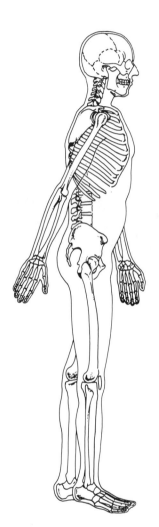

SKELETON

Terminology

This workbook has been written with a minimum of technical terminology. It is necessary, however, to employ certain basic terms in the study of anatomy. Below is an alphabetical listing of all such "technical" terms and words used in this workbook, together with their definitions.

TERM	DEFINITION
Abduct	To pull away from the middle line of the body, bone, muscle.
Adduct	To pull toward the middle line of body, bone, muscle.
Aponeurosis	A sheet like or flat tendon that covers a muscle or attaches it its insertion.
Cartilage	Connective tissue which ossifies with aging.
Cervical	Pertaining to neck.
Condyle	A rounded projection at the end of a bone.
Costal	Pertaining to ribs.
Crest	A ridge on a bone.
Distal	Furthest from the origin.
Epicondyle	A projection near the head or condyle of a bone.
Extend	To straighten out (at joint).
Fascia	Fibrous tissue enclosing muscles.
Flex	Bend (at joint).
Fossa	Depressions in a bone surface.
Iliac	Of the ilium.
Inguinal ligament	A tendon between upper front iliac spine and pubic tubercle.
Insertion	The site of a muscle's attachment to the bone that it moves.
Ischial	Of the ischium.
Interosseus	Between Bones.
Lateral	Of the side situated from the farther middle line.
Lumbar	Of the back section between the ribs and pelvis.
Medial	Of the middle. Situated closer to the middle line.
Oculi	Of the eye.
Origin	The site of a muscle's attachment to bone(s) that are fixed.
Oris	Of the mouth.
Ovate	Egg shaped.

Palmar	Of the palm side of hand.
Plantar	Of the bottom side of foot.
Process	Projection of a bone.
Pronate	To turn hand and forearm palm side down.
Proximal	Nearest to the origin.
Ramus	A process of a bone.
Sheath	Connective tissue covering.
Slip	Narrow section of a muscle.
Spine (of)	A pointed projection or process of a bone.
Spinal	Of the spine.
Styloid	A slender and pointed process of a bone.
Supinate	To turn hand and forearm palm side up.
Symphysis	Joining of two similar bones on either side of midline.
Tendon	Fibrous tissue that connects a muscle to its bony attachment.
Thoracic	Of the chest.
Transverse	At right angles to main line of a bone.
Trochanter	A large bony process at upper section of femur.
Tuberosity	Protuberance at end of a bone for attachment of a muscle.
Vertebral	Of a vertebra.

LIST OF BONES WITH COMMON NAMES

All bones listed below should be filled in on at least one of the 3 skeletal drawings to be completed on pages 67, 69, 71. See pages 7, 8, 9, for completed skeletons.

ANATOMICAL NAMES . . . . .COMMON NAMES

Head
Cranium . . . . .Skull
Frontalis . . . . Forehead
Mandible . . . . .Lower jaw
Mastoid Process
Maxilla . . . . .Upper jaw
Nasal . . . . .Nose
Occipital
Parietal . . . . Top of Head
Sphenoid
Temporal. . . . . .Temple
Zygomatic. . . . . Cheek Bone
Zygomatic Arch

Neck
Hyoid
Torso
Clavicle . . . . Collar Bone
Coccyx . . . . Tail Bones

Rib Cage
    7 True ribs   (connected by cartilage directly to breast bone)
    3 False ribs   (connected by cartilage to rib above them)
    2 Floating ribs   (front end not attached)

Sacrum

Scapula . . . . .Shoulder Blade
    Spine of scapula
    Acromion process
    Coronoid process

Spine
    7 Cervical Vertebrae . . . . Neck Vertebrae
      Cervical Vertebra   1—Atlas
      Cervical Vertebra   2—Axis
    12 Thoracic Vertebrae. . . . . .Chest Vertebrae
    5 Lumbar Vertebrae . . . . Lower back Vertebrae

Sternum . . . . Breast Bone

5

Manubrium . . . . Handle
Body . . . . Blade
Xiphoid process . . . . Point

Hip
Ilium
Ischium
Pubis

Arm
Humerus . . . . Upper Arm Bone
Radius . . . .⎫
Ulna . . . .⎬ Lower arm bone
⎭

Wrist
Carpal Bones . . . . Wrist Bones

1. Capitate	5. Minor Multiangular
2. Hamate	6. Navicular
3. Lunate	7. Pisiform
4. Major Multiangular	8. Triquetrum

Hand
Metacarpals—5 . . . . Hand Bones
Phalanges—14 . . . . Finger Bones

Leg
Femur . . . . Upper Leg Bone
Patella . . . . Knee Cap
Tibia . . . . Shin Bone
Fibula

Ankle
Tarsal Bones . . . . Ankle Bones

1. Calcaneus . . . . Heel bone	5. Cuneiform III
2. Cuboid	6. Navicular
3. Cuneiform I	7. Talus
4. Cuneiform II	

Foot
Metatarsals-5 . . . . Foot Bones
Phalanges—14 . . . . Toe Bones

6

Skeleton — Front

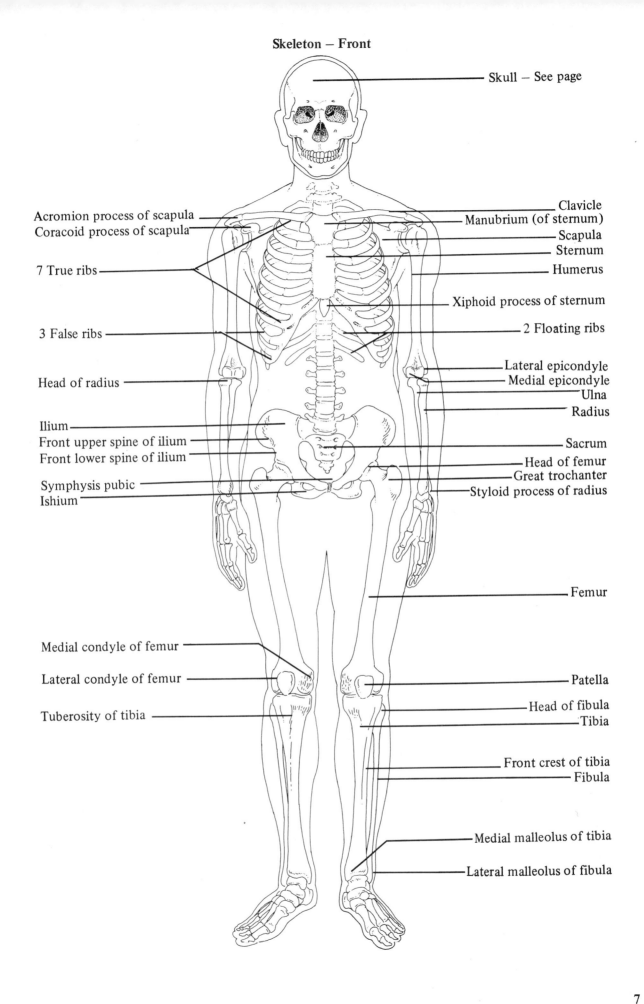

Skull — See page

Acromion process of scapula
Coracoid process of scapula

Clavicle
Manubrium (of sternum)
Scapula
Sternum
Humerus

7 True ribs

Xiphoid process of sternum

3 False ribs

2 Floating ribs

Head of radius

Lateral epicondyle
Medial epicondyle
Ulna
Radius

Ilium
Front upper spine of ilium
Front lower spine of ilium

Sacrum
Head of femur
Great trochanter
Styloid process of radius

Symphysis pubic
Ishium

Femur

Medial condyle of femur

Lateral condyle of femur

Patella

Head of fibula
Tibia

Tuberosity of tibia

Front crest of tibia
Fibula

Medial malleolus of tibia

Lateral malleolus of fibula

Skeleton — Side

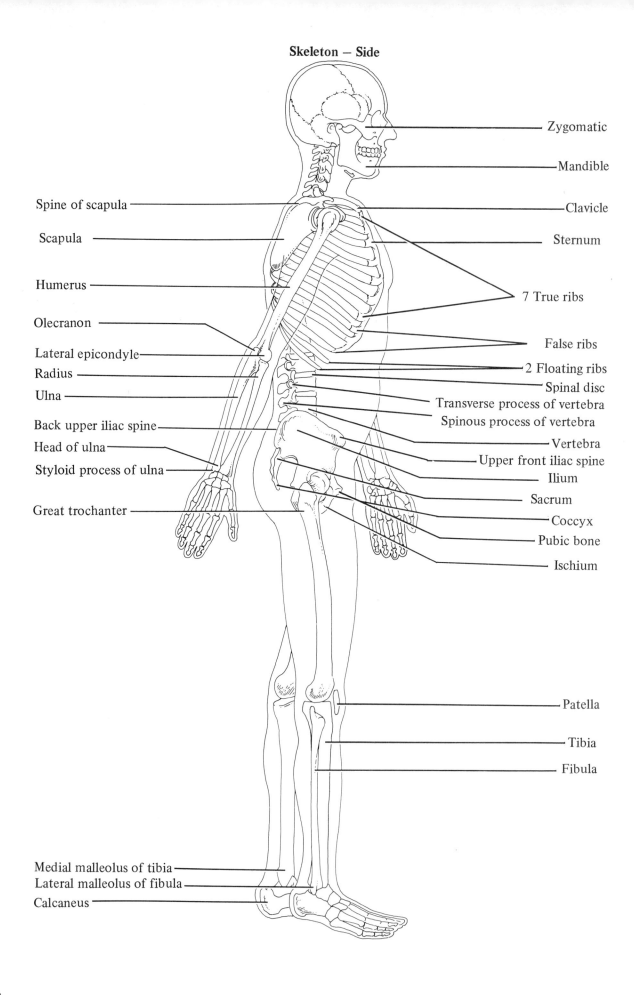

Zygomatic

Mandible

Spine of scapula

Clavicle

Scapula

Sternum

Humerus

7 True ribs

Olecranon

False ribs

Lateral epicondyle

2 Floating ribs

Radius

Spinal disc

Ulna

Transverse process of vertebra

Spinous process of vertebra

Back upper iliac spine

Vertebra

Head of ulna

Upper front iliac spine

Styloid process of ulna

Ilium

Sacrum

Great trochanter

Coccyx

Pubic bone

Ischium

Patella

Tibia

Fibula

Medial malleolus of tibia

Lateral malleolus of fibula

Calcaneus

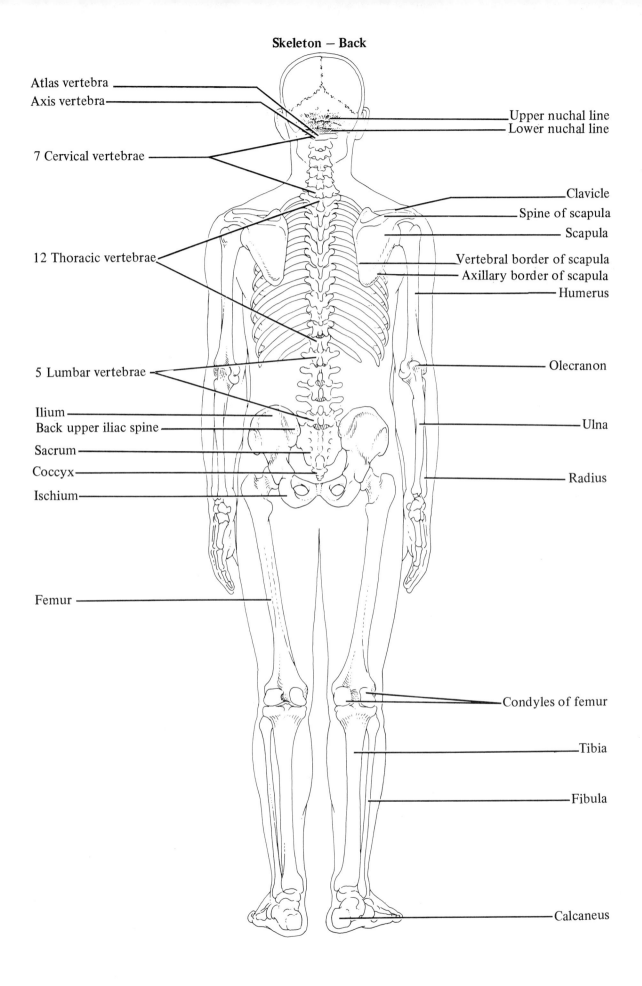

Atlas vertebra

Axis vertebra

Upper nuchal line

Lower nuchal line

7 Cervical vertebrae

Clavicle

Spine of scapula

Scapula

12 Thoracic vertebrae

Vertebral border of scapula

Axillary border of scapula

Humerus

Olecranon

5 Lumbar vertebrae

Ulna

Ilium

Back upper iliac spine

Sacrum

Coccyx

Radius

Ischium

Femur

Condyles of femur

Tibia

Fibula

Calcaneus

Male and Female Skeleton Comparison

MALE   **FEMALE**

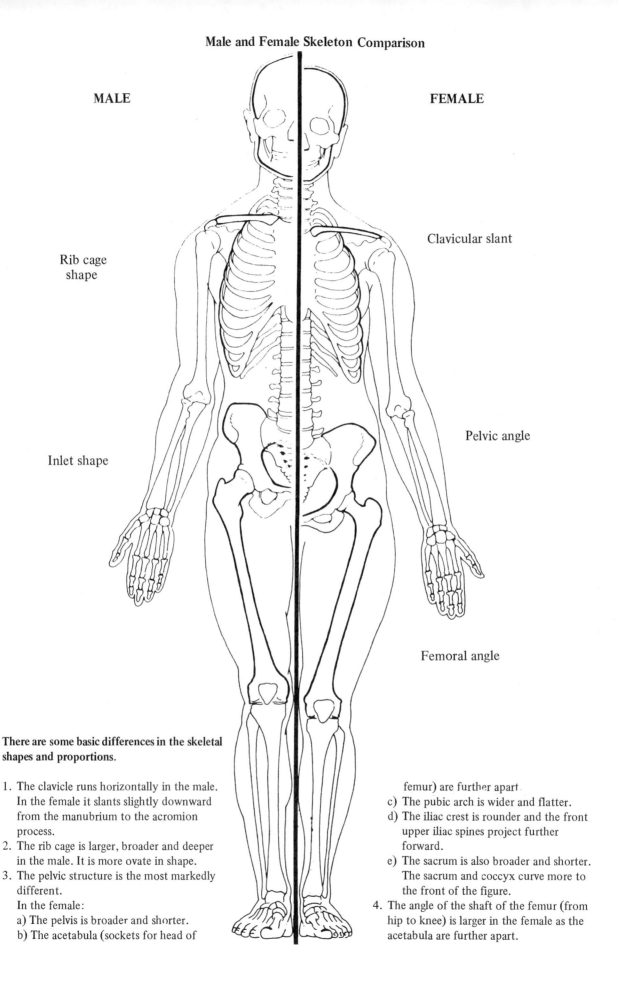

Clavicular slant

Rib cage
shape

Pelvic angle

Inlet shape

Femoral angle

There are some basic differences in the skeletal shapes and proportions.

1. The clavicle runs horizontally in the male. In the female it slants slightly downward from the manubrium to the acromion process.
2. The rib cage is larger, broader and deeper in the male. It is more ovate in shape.
3. The pelvic structure is the most markedly different.
   In the female:
   a) The pelvis is broader and shorter.
   b) The acetabula (sockets for head of

femur) are further apart.
   c) The pubic arch is wider and flatter.
   d) The iliac crest is rounder and the front upper iliac spines project further forward.
   e) The sacrum is also broader and shorter. The sacrum and coccyx curve more to the front of the figure.
4. The angle of the shaft of the femur (from hip to knee) is larger in the female as the acetabula are further apart.

10

Skull

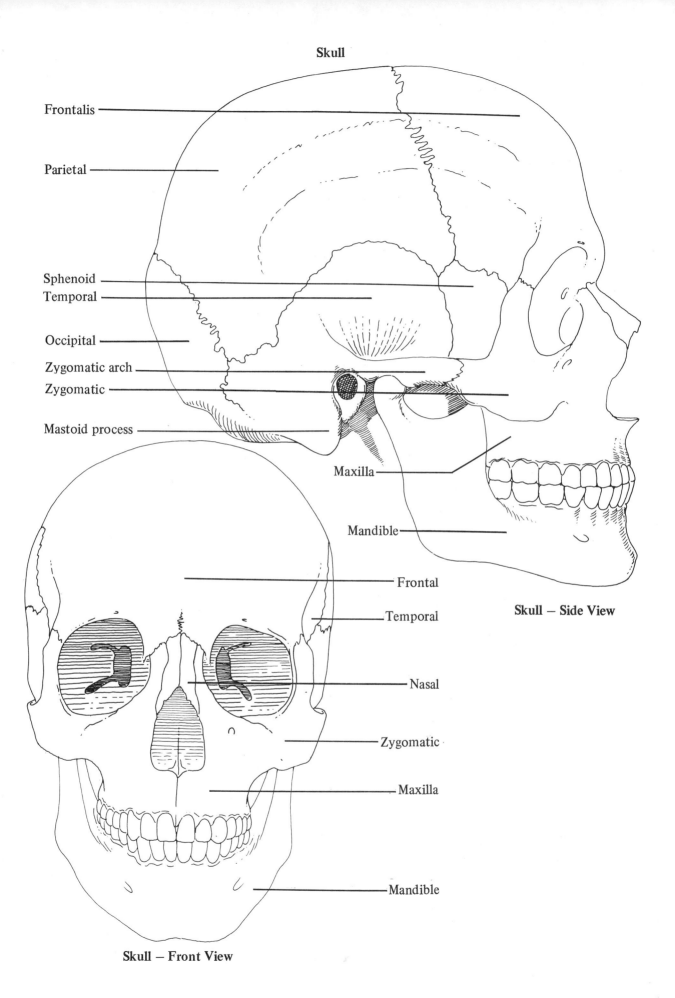

Frontalis

Parietal

Sphenoid

Temporal

Occipital

Zygomatic arch

Zygomatic

Mastoid process

Maxilla

Mandible

Skull — Side View

Frontal

Temporal

Nasal

Zygomatic

Maxilla

Mandible

Skull — Front View

Neck — Bone Structure

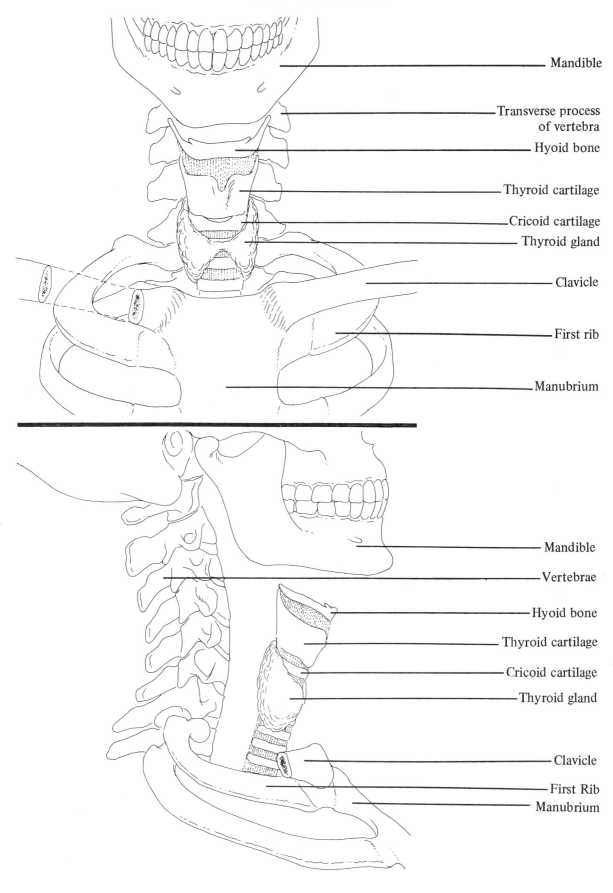

Mandible

Transverse process
of vertebra

Hyoid bone

Thyroid cartilage

Cricoid cartilage

Thyroid gland

Clavicle

First rib

Manubrium

Mandible

Vertebrae

Hyoid bone

Thyroid cartilage

Cricoid cartilage

Thyroid gland

Clavicle

First Rib

Manubrium

Hand and Wrist — Bone Structure

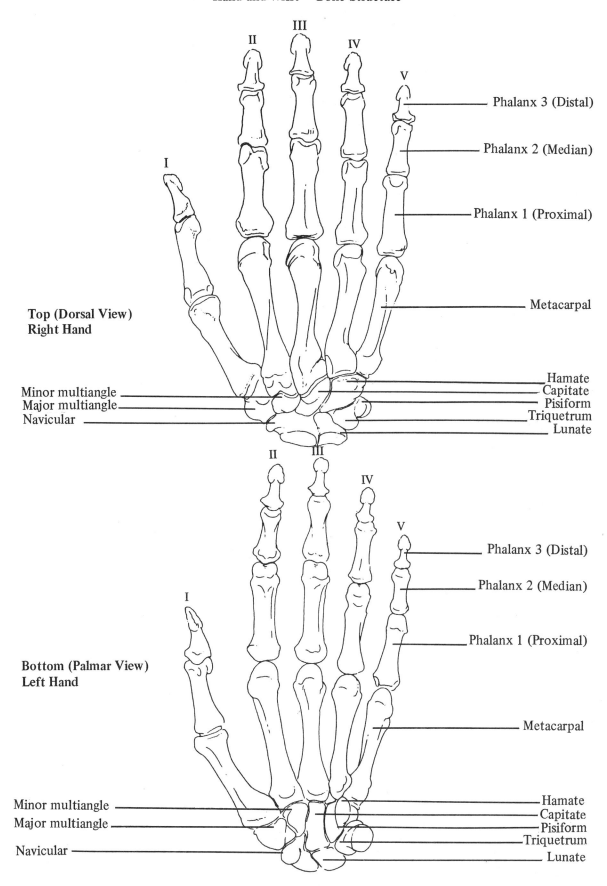

II   III   IV

V

I

— Phalanx 3 (Distal)

— Phalanx 2 (Median)

— Phalanx 1 (Proximal)

**Top (Dorsal View)
Right Hand**

— Metacarpal

Minor multiangle ———
Major multiangle ———
Navicular ———

——— Hamate
——— Capitate
——— Pisiform
——— Triquetrum
——— Lunate

II   III   IV

V

I

— Phalanx 3 (Distal)

— Phalanx 2 (Median)

— Phalanx 1 (Proximal)

**Bottom (Palmar View)
Left Hand**

— Metacarpal

Minor multiangle ———
Major multiangle ———
Navicular ———

——— Hamate
——— Capitate
——— Pisiform
——— Triquetrum
——— Lunate

13

Foot and Ankle – Bone Structure

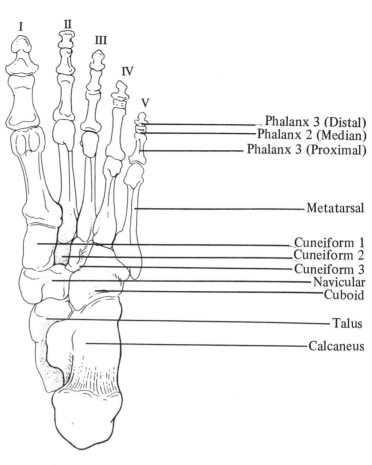

I II III IV V

Phalanx 3 (Distal)
Phalanx 2 (Median)
Phalanx 3 (Proximal)

Metatarsal

Cuneiform 1
Cuneiform 2
Cuneiform 3
Navicular
Cuboid

Talus

Calcaneus

**Bottom(Plantar View)
Left Foot**

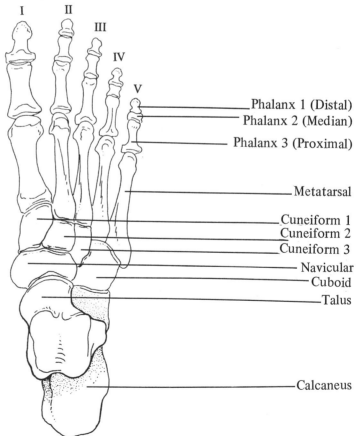

I II III IV V

Phalanx 1 (Distal)
Phalanx 2 (Median)
Phalanx 3 (Proximal)

Metatarsal

Cuneiform 1
Cuneiform 2
Cuneiform 3
Navicular
Cuboid
Talus

Calcaneus

**Top (Dorsal View)
Right Foot**

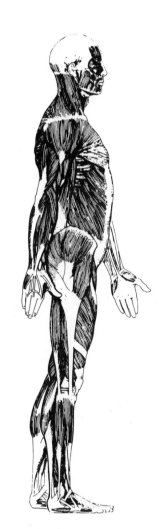

MUSCLES

Muscle Action

Muscles are composed of areas of tissue which contract when chemically activated. When a muscle contracts it shortens and pulls on the bone into which it is inserted. As a muscle pulls it moves the particular bone, by bending, straightening, or rotating it.

The muscle also bulks up as it contracts thus changing its shape. This is illustrated in the diagram of the Biceps muscle below in :
  a) the Biceps is in its extended position and the arm is straight.
  b) the Biceps is activated and the forearm has been bent at the elbow joint towards the shoulder. Notice how the biceps has become bulky towards the upper part of the arm.

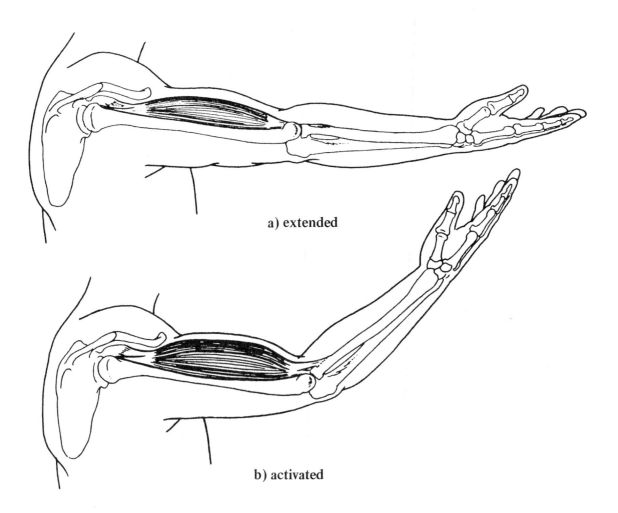

a) extended

b) activated

Front — Complete Musculature

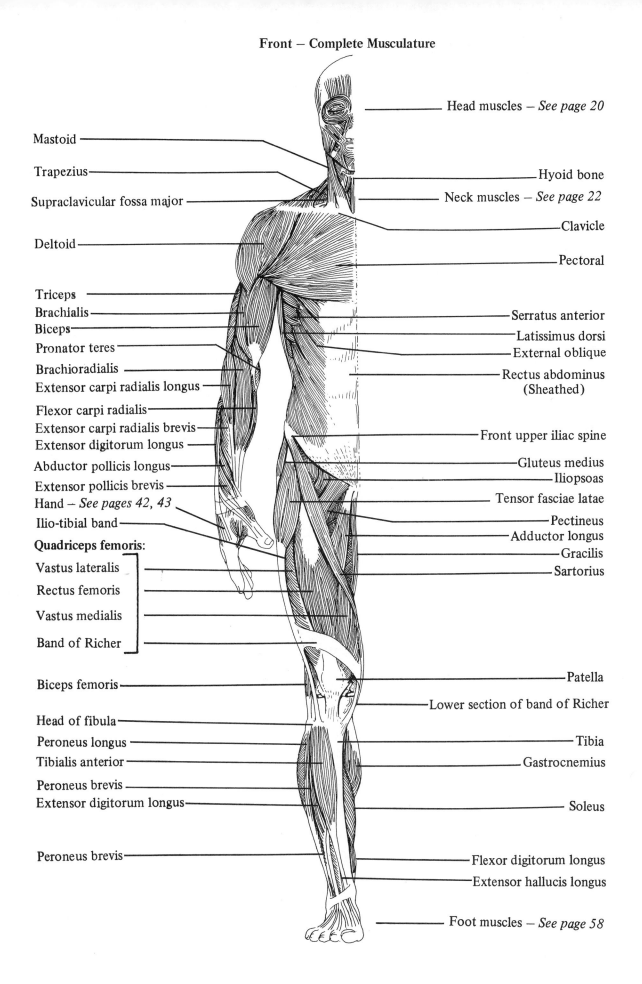

Head muscles – *See page 20*

Mastoid

Trapezius

Supraclavicular fossa major

Deltoid

Triceps
Brachialis
Biceps
Pronator teres
Brachioradialis
Extensor carpi radialis longus
Flexor carpi radialis
Extensor carpi radialis brevis
Extensor digitorum longus
Abductor pollicis longus
Extensor pollicis brevis
Hand – *See pages 42, 43*
Ilio-tibial band

Quadriceps femoris:

Vastus lateralis

Rectus femoris

Vastus medialis

Band of Richer

Biceps femoris

Head of fibula
Peroneus longus
Tibialis anterior
Peroneus brevis
Extensor digitorum longus

Peroneus brevis

Hyoid bone
Neck muscles – *See page 22*
Clavicle
Pectoral

Serratus anterior
Latissimus dorsi
External oblique
Rectus abdominus
(Sheathed)

Front upper iliac spine

Gluteus medius
Iliopsoas
Tensor fasciae latae
Pectineus
Adductor longus
Gracilis
Sartorius

Patella
Lower section of band of Richer

Tibia
Gastrocnemius

Soleus

Flexor digitorum longus
Extensor hallucis longus

Foot muscles – *See page 58*

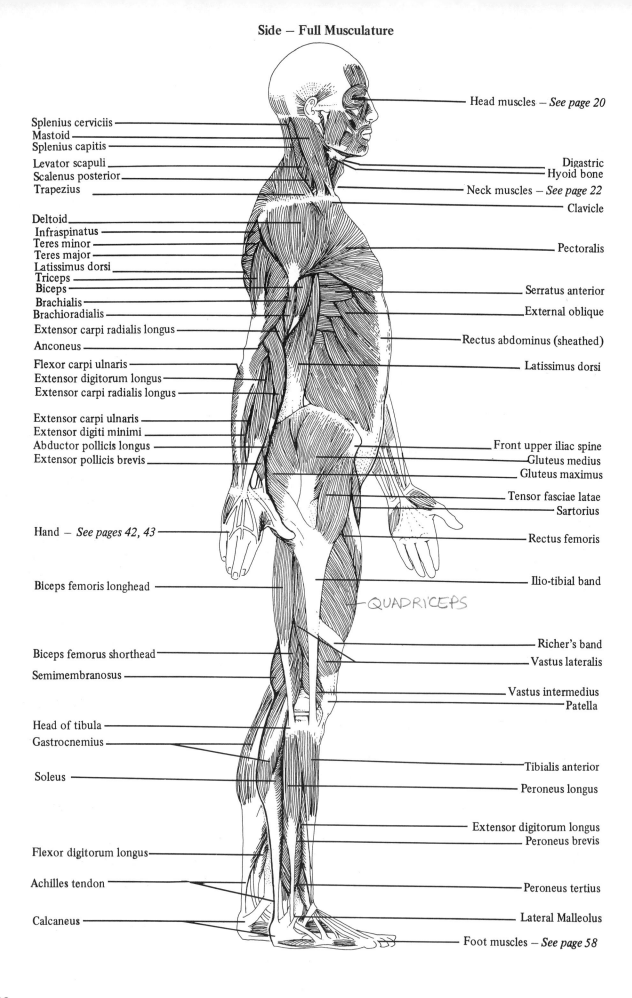

Head muscles — *See page 20*

Splenius cerviciis
Mastoid
Splenius capitis

Digastric
Hyoid bone

Levator scapuli
Scalenus posterior
Trapezius

Neck muscles — *See page 22*

Clavicle

Deltoid
Infraspinatus
Teres minor
Teres major
Latissimus dorsi
Triceps
Biceps
Brachialis
Brachioradialis

Pectoralis

Serratus anterior

External oblique

Extensor carpi radialis longus

Rectus abdominus (sheathed)

Anconeus

Latissimus dorsi

Flexor carpi ulnaris
Extensor digitorum longus
Extensor carpi radialis longus

Extensor carpi ulnaris
Extensor digiti minimi
Abductor pollicis longus
Extensor pollicis brevis

Front upper iliac spine
Gluteus medius
Gluteus maximus

Tensor fasciae latae
Sartorius

Hand — *See pages 42, 43*

Rectus femoris

Ilio-tibial band

Biceps femoris longhead

QUADRICEPS

Richer's band

Biceps femorus shorthead

Vastus lateralis

Semimembranosus

Vastus intermedius
Patella

Head of tibula
Gastrocnemius

Tibialis anterior

Soleus

Peroneus longus

Extensor digitorum longus
Peroneus brevis

Flexor digitorum longus

Achilles tendon

Peroneus tertius

Calcaneus

Lateral Malleolus

Foot muscles — *See page 58*

Back — Complete Musculature

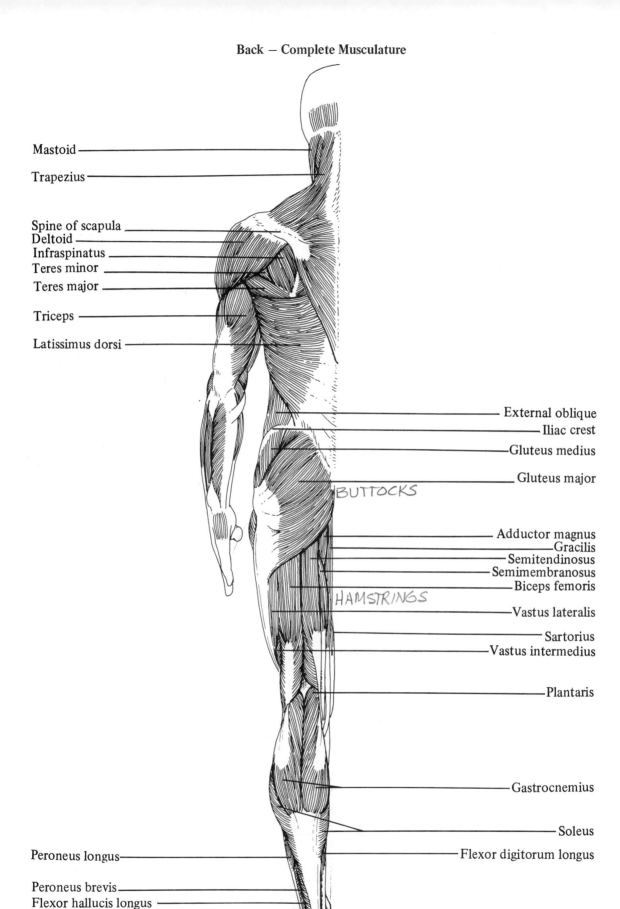

Mastoid

Trapezius

Spine of scapula
Deltoid
Infraspinatus
Teres minor
Teres major

Triceps

Latissimus dorsi

External oblique
Iliac crest
Gluteus medius
Gluteus major

BUTTOCKS

Adductor magnus
Gracilis
Semitendinosus
Semimembranosus
Biceps femoris
Vastus lateralis
Sartorius
Vastus intermedius

HAMSTRINGS

Plantaris

Gastrocnemius

Soleus

Flexor digitorum longus

Peroneus longus

Peroneus brevis
Flexor hallucis longus

Achilles tendon
Calcaneus

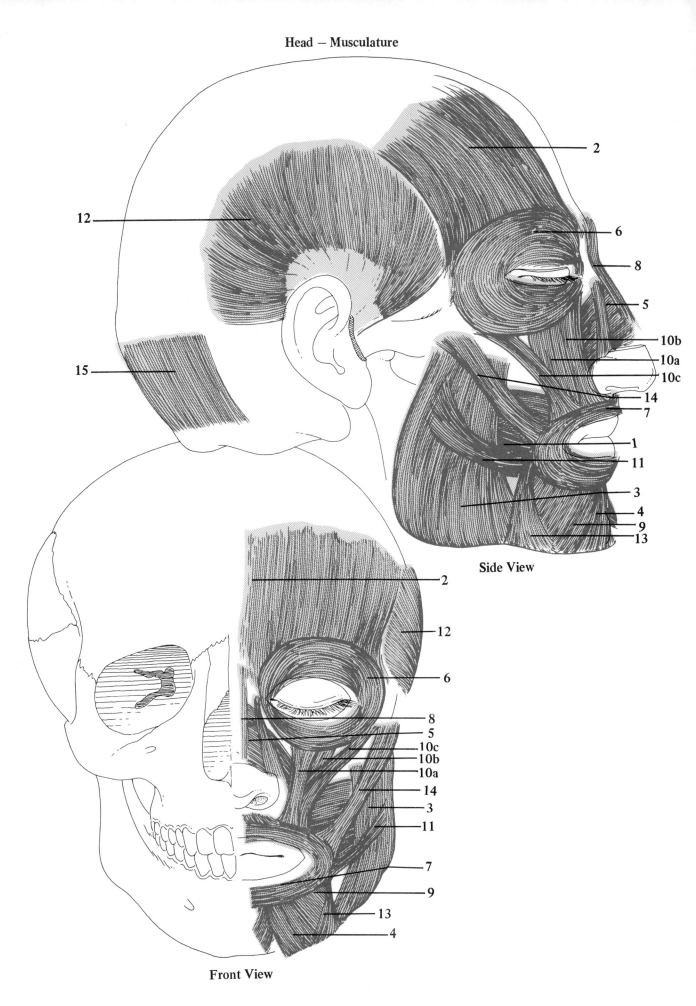

12

2

6

8

5

10b
10a
10c

15

14

7

1

11

3
4
9
13

Side View

2

12

6

8
5
10c
10b
10a
14
3
11

7

9

13

4

Front View

MUSCLES OF THE HEAD

	Name	Action
1.	Buccinator	Draws corner of mouth laterally.
2.	Frontalis	Elevates eyebrow and wrinkles forehead.
3.	Masseter	Raises Mandible.
4.	Mentalis	Raises skin of chin and protrudes lower lip.
5.	Nasalis	Pulls down wing of nose.
6.	Orbicularis Oculi	Closes eye.
7.	Orbicularis Oris	Closes mouth
8.	Procerus	Wrinkles skin of nose.
9.	Quadratus Labii Inferioris	Pulls lower lip out and down.
10.	Quadratus Labii Superioris	Composed of 3 slips.
	a) Infraorbital Head	Raises upper lip.
	b) Angular Head	Raises upper lip and wing of nose.
	c) Zygomaticus Minor	Raises corner of mouth.
11.	Risorius	Pulls corner of mouth laterally.
12.	Temporalis	Pulls mandible up.
13.	Triangularis	Pulls corner of mouth down.
14.	Zygomaticus	Pulls corner of mouth up and laterally.
15.	Occipital	Stretches scalp.

The following are the larger muscles of the head.
These have been listed with their orgins, insertions and actions.

Name	Frontalis
Origin	Top of nasal bone and arch of eye socket.
Insertion	Front edge of cranial aponeurosis
Action	Elevates eye and brow and wrinkles forehead

Name	Orbicularis Oris
Origin	Muscle around mouth
Insertion	Into skin of lips
Action	Closes mouth

Name	Masseter
Origin	Lower edge of zygomatic arch
Insertion	Rear anble of mandible
Action	Raises mandible

Name	Temporalis
Origin	Pemporal bone
Insertion	Top front of mandible
Action	Raises mandible

Name	Orbicularis Oculi
Origin	Around eye socket
Insertion	Eyelids
Action	Closes eye

Name	Triangularis
Origin	Lower edge of mandible
Insertion	Corner of mouth
Action	Draws corner of mouth down

Neck Musculature

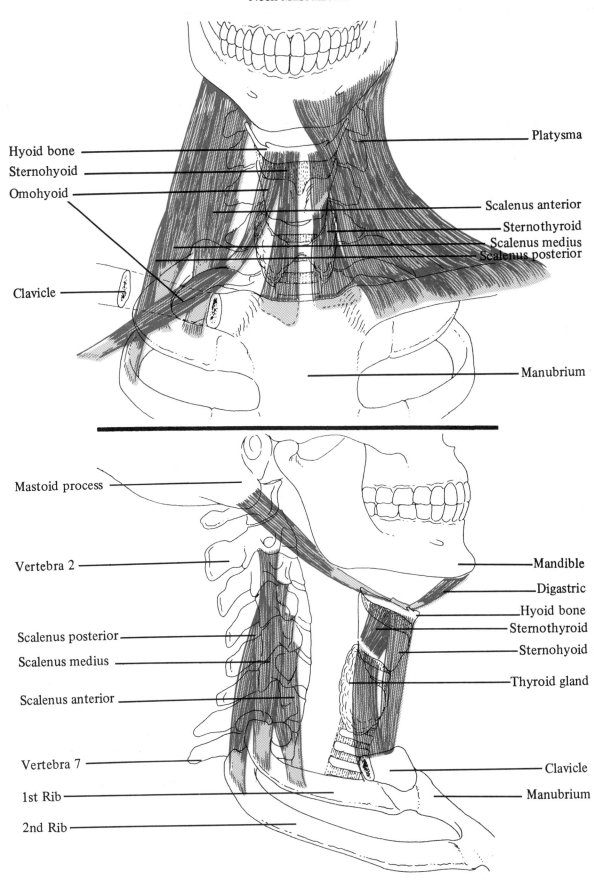

Platysma

Hyoid bone

Sternohyoid

Omohyoid

Scalenus anterior

Sternothyroid

Scalenus medius

Scalenus posterior

Clavicle

Manubrium

Mastoid process

Vertebra 2

Mandible

Digastric

Hyoid bone

Sternothyroid

Sternohyoid

Thyroid gland

Scalenus posterior

Scalenus medius

Scalenus anterior

Vertebra 7

Clavicle

1st Rib

Manubrium

2nd Rib

MUSCLES OF THE NECK

Name	**Platysma**
Origin	Fascia of pectoral and deltoid muscles.
Insertion	Facial skin and lower border of mandible.
Action	Stretches skin of neck.

Name	**Digastric (A Jaw Muscle)**
Origin	Mastoid process
Insertion	Hyoid bone
Action	Pulls mandible down with fixed hyoid bone.
	Pulls hyoid up with fixed mandible.

Name	**Omohyoid**
Origin	Upper surface of scapula.
Insertion	Hyoid bone.
Action	Pulls hyoid down and back.

Name	**Sternohyoid**
Origin	Rear surface of manubrium
Insertion	Hyoid bone.
Action	Pulls hyoid down.

Name	**Sternothyroid**
Origin	Rear surface of manubrium
Insertion	Thyroid cartilage
Action	Pulls thyroid cartilage down

Name	**Thyrohyoid**
Origin	Thyroid cartilage
Insertion	Hyoid bone
Action	Pulls hyoid and thyroid cartilage together

Name	**Scalenus (Anterior, Medius, Posterior — 3 Muscles)**
Origin	Cervical vertebrae II to VII
Insertion	Top surface of first 2 ribs
Action	Elevate the first 2 ribs

Other neck muscles are the Mylohyoid and Stylohyoid.

Torso – Musculature

Front   Side   Back

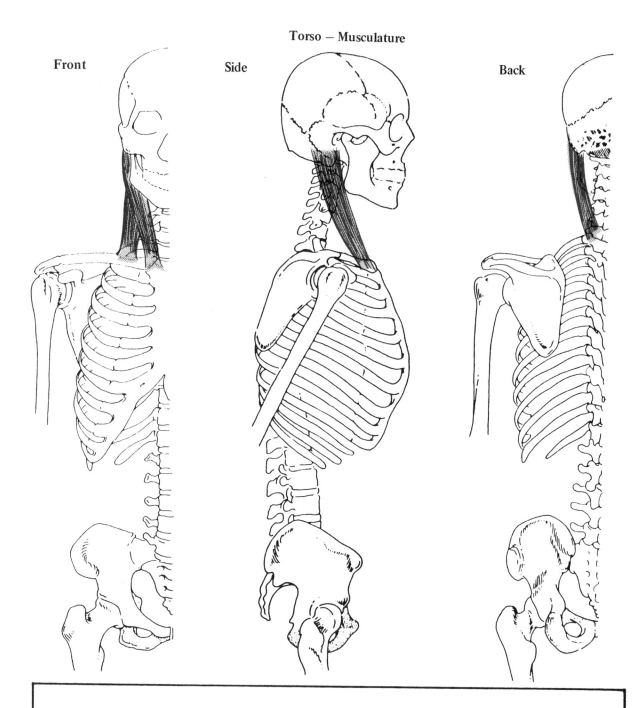

Name	**Sternocleidomastoid**
Origin	Middle head from the front surface of manubrium of sternum.
	Side head from the sternal end of clavicle.
Insertion	Through common tendon into mastoid process.
Action	When one side is contracted the head is rotated to opposite side.
	When both sides contract, the chin is raised and head is tilted back.

Front   Side   Back

Name	Pectoralis Major
Origin	From most of the clavicle and the entire front surface of the sternum down to the 6th costal cartilage.
Insertion	Ridge on upper front of humerus.
Action	Pulls arm down, towards front of chest and rotates it inwardly.

Front   Side   Back

Name	**Serratus Anterior**
Origin	Through nine slips from the outer surface of the upper eight ribs.
Insertion	Vertebral border of scapula (goes underneath scapula).
Action	Pulls scapula forward and against the rib cage.

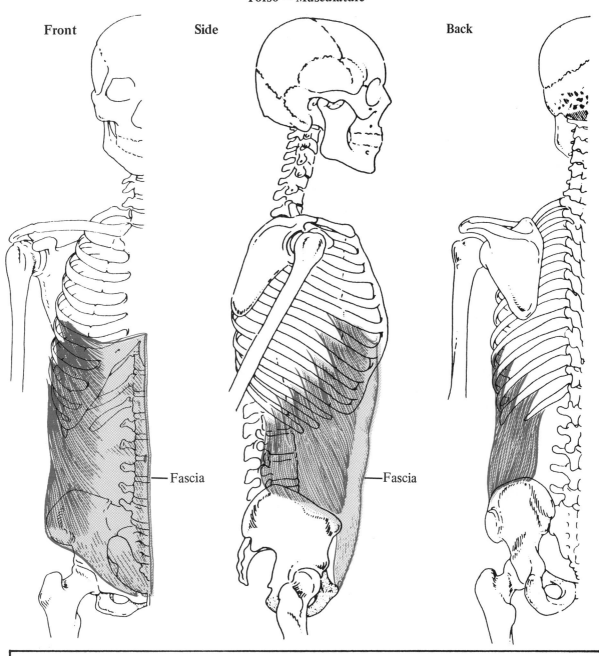

Front   Side   Back

—Fascia   —Fascia

Name	External Oblique
Origin	Through eight slips from the lower eight ribs.
Insertion	Iliac crest, rectus abdominus sheath and the inguinal ligament.
Action	Compresses abdominal cavity. Each pulls chest to its own side.

Front   Side   Back

Name	**Rectus Abdominus**
Origin	Pubic crest
Insertion	Outer surface and lower edge of 5th to 7th costal cartilages.
Action	Compress abdominal cavity, with fixed pelvis, muscles bend trunk forward.

Note: The vertical depression between the 2 muscles is called the "Linea Alba".

Front   Side   Back

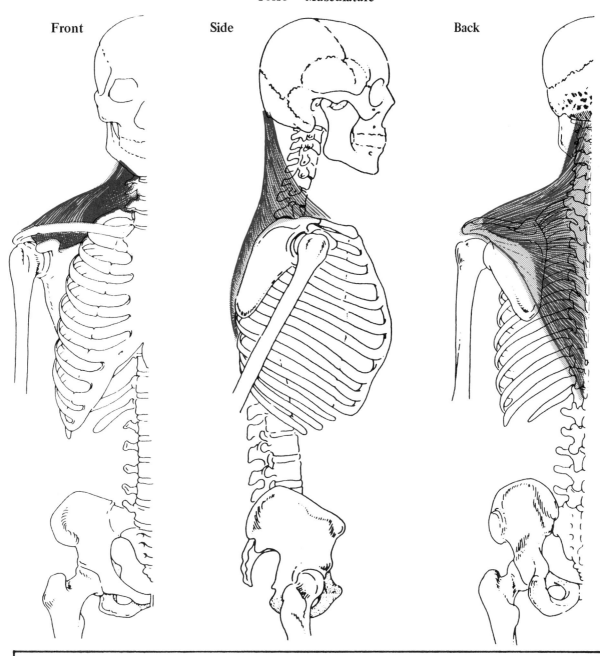

Name	**Trapezius**
Origin	Upper nuchal line of the occipital bone; the spinal processes of all the neck and chest vertebrae.
Insertion	Outer third of clavicle, acromion process and spine of scapula.
Action	Pulls scapula towards spine; helps in raising arm by rotating scapula.

Front   **Side**   **Back**

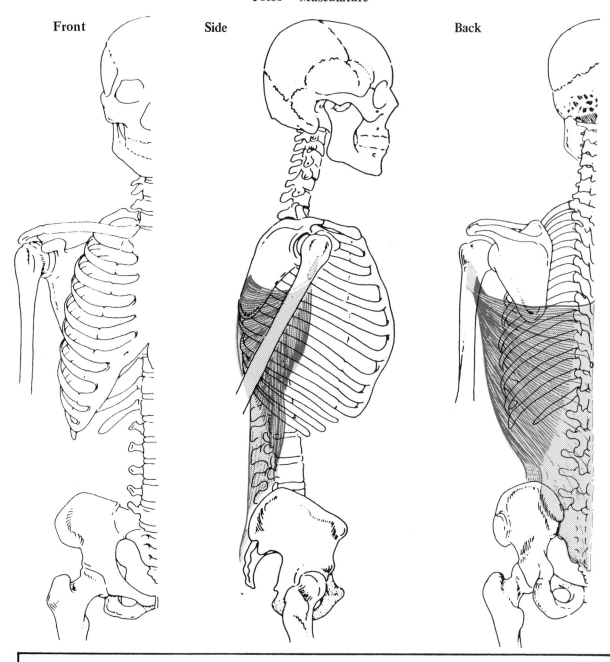

Name	**Latissimus Dorsi**
Origin	From the spinal process of the lower 7 chest vertebrae, the lumbar vertebrae and the sacrum; the iliac crest; and through 4 slips from the lower 4 ribs.
Insertion	Front, near top of humerus
Action	Pulls arm down and back; rotates arm inwardly.

Torso — Musculature

Front   Side   Back

Semispinalis capitis

Erector spinae

Name	**Erector Spinae - A group of muscles**
Origin	Crest of ilium, sacrum and various processes of the lumbar and thoracic vertebrae.
Insertion	By various slips into the ribs, and processes of the spine. The semispinalis capitis into the occipital bone.
Action	Straighten the spine and bend it backwards. Upper section (semispinalis capitis) extends the head.

31

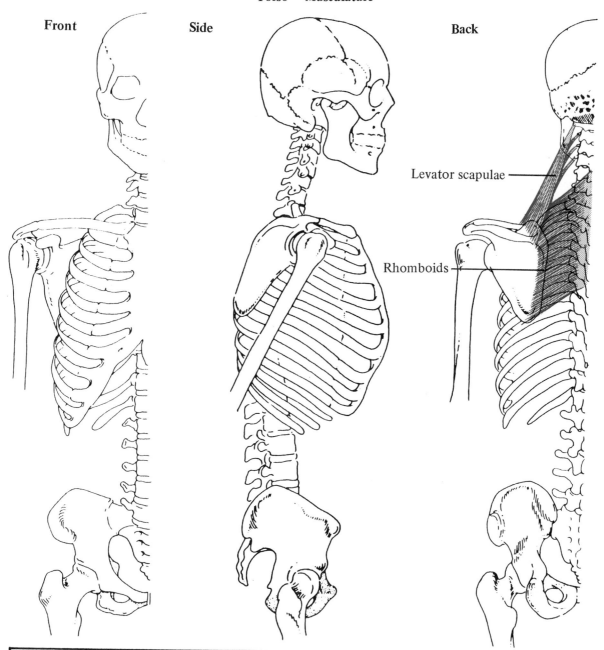

Front Side Back

Levator scapulae

Rhomboids

Name	**Rhomboids (Major and Minor)**
Origin	Major-Spinal processes of chest vertebrae I to IV.
	Minor-Spinal processes of chest vertebrae VI and VII.
Insertion	Vertebra edge of scapula.
Action	Pulls scapula up and towards spine.

Name	**Levator scapulae**
Origin	Through 4 slips from the transverse processes of cervical vertebrae I through IV.
Insertion	Upper angle of scapula.
Action	Raises scapula

Torso — Musculature

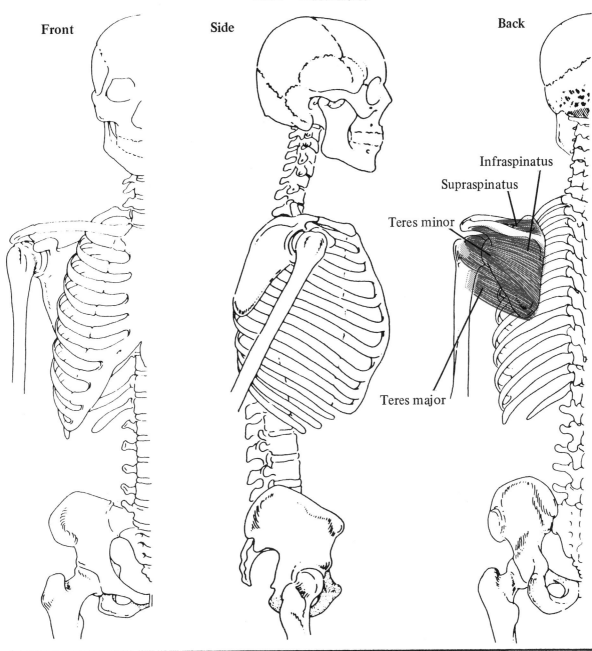

Front

Side

Back

Infraspinatus

Supraspinatus

Teres minor

Teres major

Name	Teres Minor	Name	Supraspinatus
Origin	Middle of outer border of scapula.	Origin	Supraspinous fossa of scapula.
Insertion	Greater tuberosity of humerous	Insertion	Greater tuberosity of humerus.
Action	Adducts arm; rotates it outwardly.	Action	Raises arm sideways; rotates it outwardly.

Name	Teres Major	Name	Infraspinatus
Origin	Lower angle of scapula	Origin	Infraspinous fossa of scapula.
Insertion	Upper medial surface of humerus.	Insertion	Greater tuberosity of humerus.
Action	Lowers arm and rotates it inwardly.	Action	Raises arm sideways.

Torso — Musculature

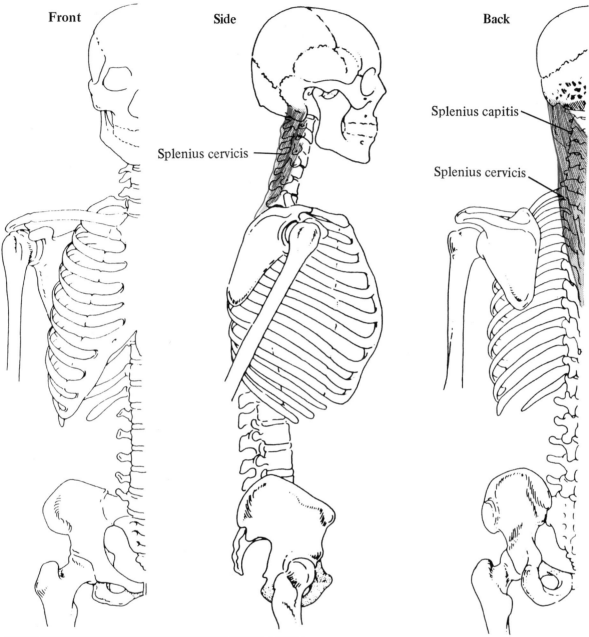

Front   Side   Back

Splenius cervicis

Splenius capitis

Splenius cervicis

Name	**Splenius Capitis**
Origin	Spinal processes from 3rd neck to 3rd chest vertebrae.
Insertion	Upper nuchal line of occipital bone.
Action	Pulls neck back and sideways.

Name	**Splenius Cervicis**
Origin	Spinal processes of 3rd to 6th chest vertebrae.
Insertion	Side processes of first 3 neck vertebrae.
Action	Pulls neck back and sideways.

Arm – Musculature

Front

Outside

Back

Inside

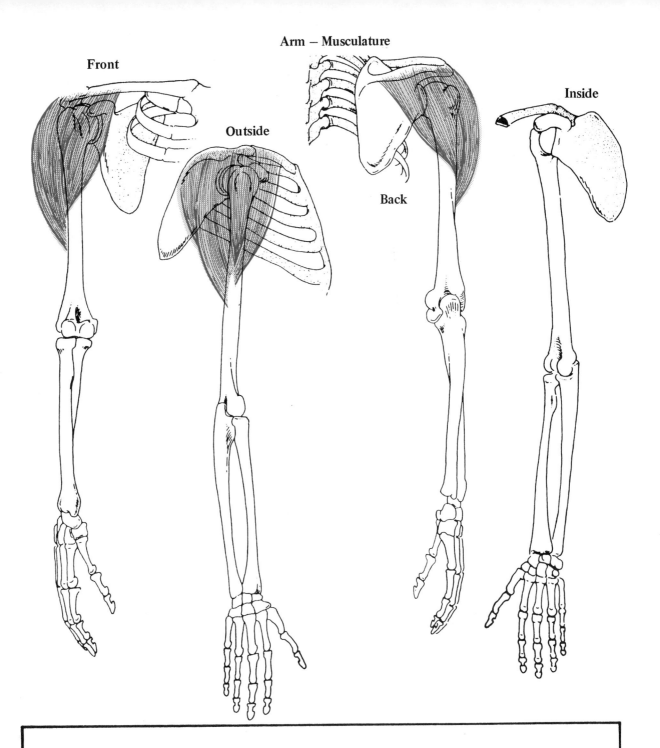

Name	**Deltoid**
Origin	Lower edge of spine of scapula, outer edge of acromion, process and lower edge of lateral end of clavicle.
Insertion	Middle of outside of humerus.
Action	Raises the arm.

Arm – Musculature

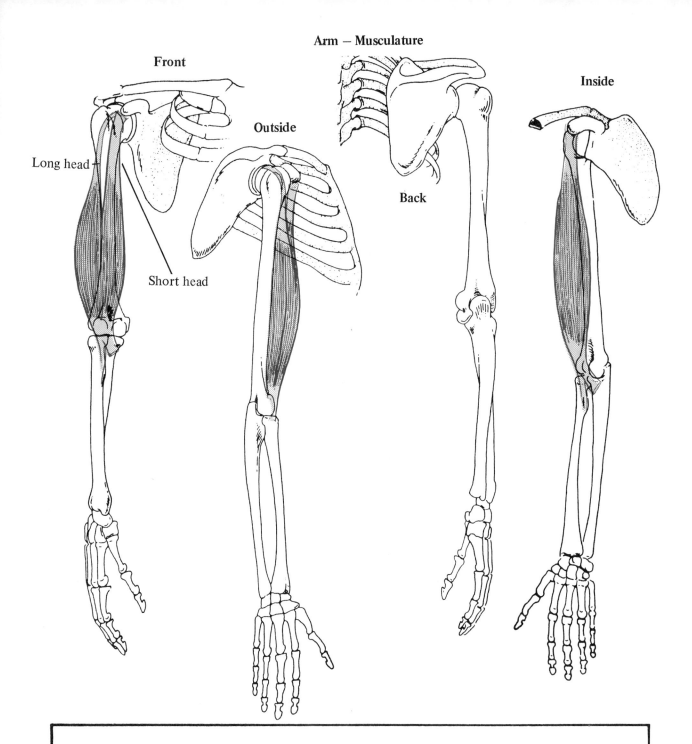

Front

Long head

Short head

Outside

Back

Inside

Name	Biceps
Origin	Short head from coracoid process.
	Long head from glenoid fossa.
Insertion	Tuberosity of radius.
Action	Flexes and supinates forearm.

Arm – Musculature

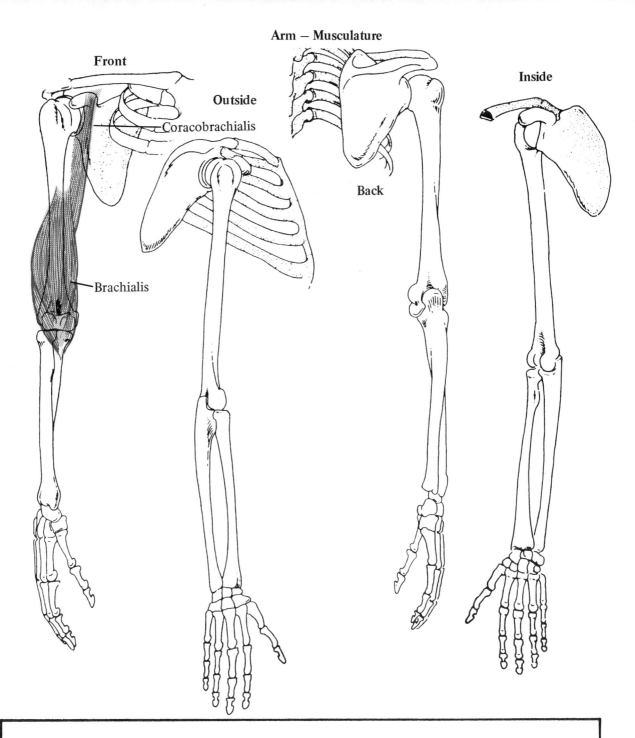

Front

Outside

Coracobrachialis

Back

Inside

Brachialis

Name	Coracobrachialis
Origin	Coracoid process.
Insertion	Medial edge of humerus.
Action	Raises arm.

Name	Brachialis
Origin	Front of humerus.
Insertion	Tuberosity of ulna.
Action	Flexes forearm.

37

Arm – Musculature

Front

Outside

Inside

Back

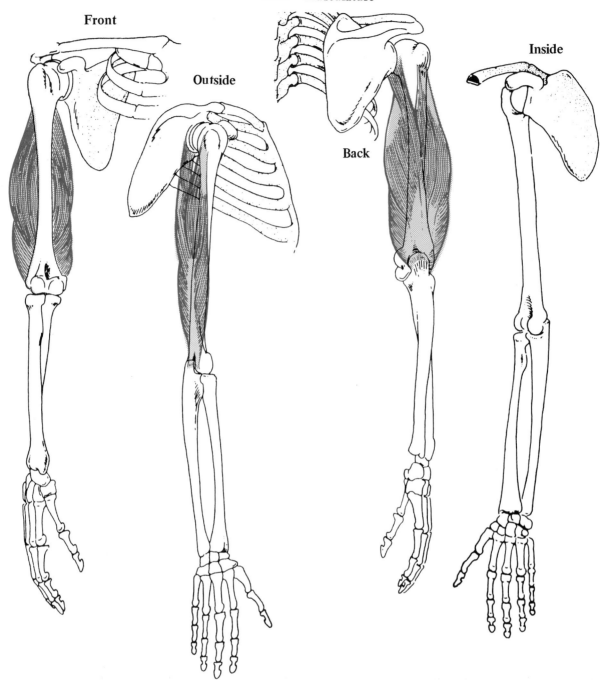

Name	Triceps
Origin	Longhead – upper outer edge of scapula.
	Outerhead – upper outer back of humerus.
	Innerhead – Back of humerus.
Insertion	By common tendon into the olecranon of ulna.
Action	Extends forearm.

Arm — Musculature

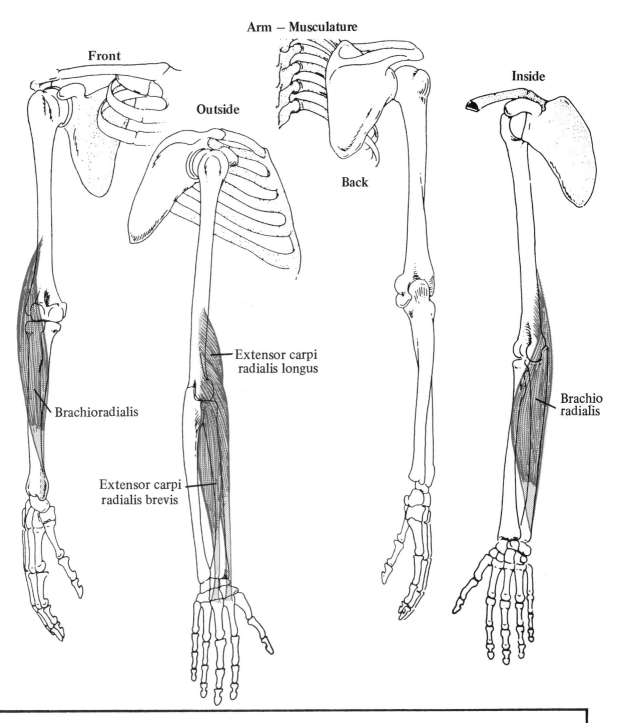

Front

Outside

Back

Inside

Extensor carpi
radialis longus

Brachioradialis

Brachio
radialis

Extensor carpi
radialis brevis

Name	Brachioradialis	Name	Extensor Carpi Radialis Brevis
Origin	Lateral ridge of epicondyle of humerus.	Origin	Lateral epicondyle of humerus.
Insertion	Styloid process of radius.	Insertion	Base of metacarpal III.
Action	Flexes and supinates forearm.	Action	Extends and abducts hand.

Name	Extensor Carpi Radialis Longus
Origin	Outer epicondyle ridge of humerus.
Insertion	Base of metacarpal II.
Action	Extends and abducts hand.

Arm – Musculature

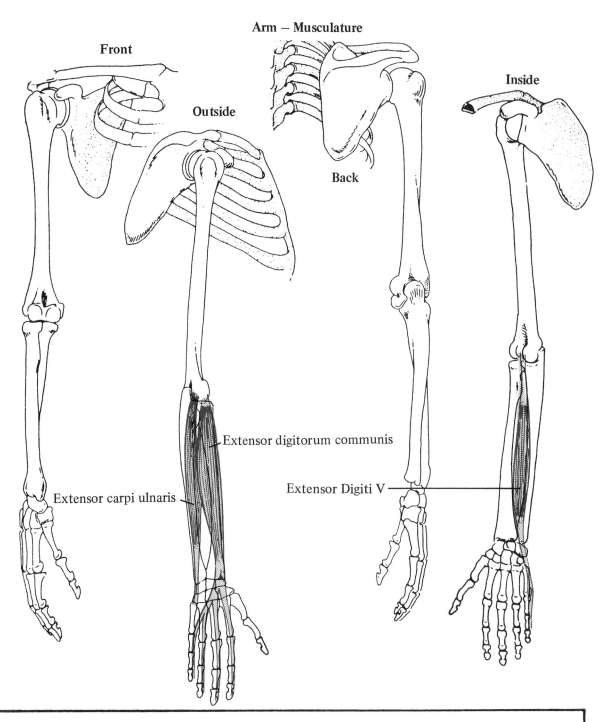

Front

Outside

Back

Inside

Extensor digitorum communis

Extensor carpi ulnaris

Extensor Digiti V

Name	Extensor Carpi Ulnaris	Name	Extensor Digiti V
Origin	Lateral epicondyle of humerus.	Origin	Lateral epicondyle of humerus.
Insertion	Base of metacarpal V.	Insertion	(with tendon of extensor digitorum communis) into 1st phalange of little finger.
Action	Extends and abducts hand.	Action	Extends 1" phalanx of little finger.

Name	Extensor Digitorum Communis
Origin	Lateral epicondyle of humerus.
Insertion	By 4 tendons to bases of phalanges of the 4 fingers.
Action	Extends and spreads fingers.

Arm — Musculature

Front

Outside

Back

Inside

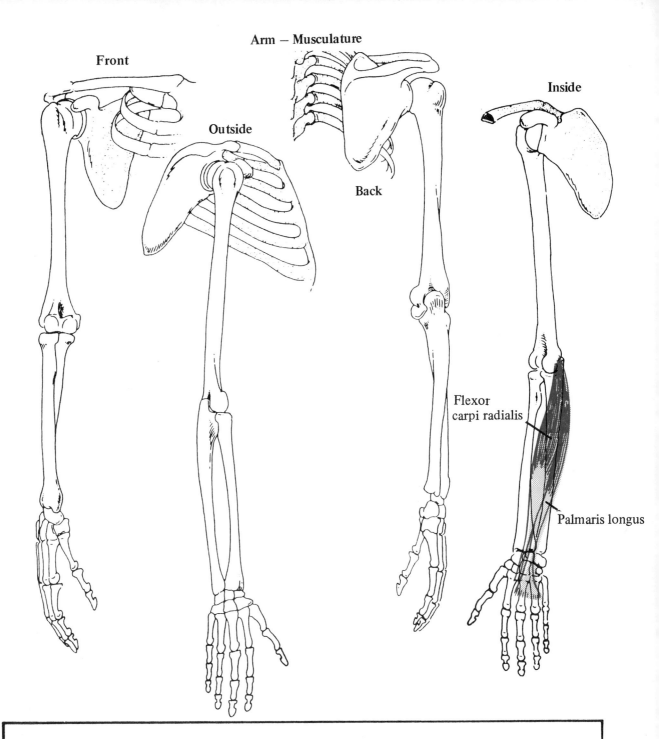

Flexor carpi radialis

Palmaris longus

Name	**Palmaris Longus**
Origin	Medial epicondyle of humerus.
Insertion	Into palmar aponeurosis.
Action	Pronates forearm and flexes hand.
Name	**Flexor Carpi Radialis**
Origin	Medial epicondyle of humerus.
Insertion	Base of metacarpal II.
Action	Flexes hand.

Arm — Transitional Musculature

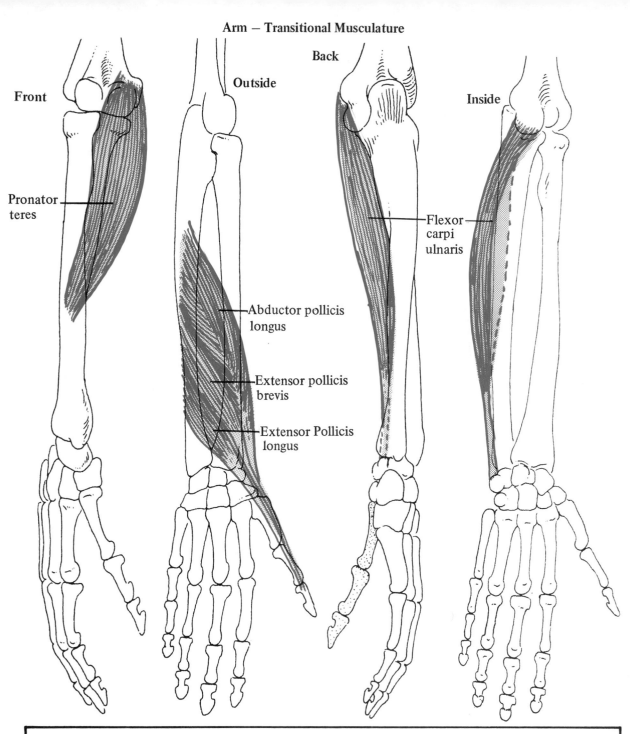

Front

Outside

Back

Inside

Pronator teres

Abductor pollicis longus

Extensor pollicis brevis

Extensor Pollicis longus

Flexor carpi ulnaris

Name	**Pronator Teres**	Name	**Extensor Pollicis Longus**
Origin	Medial epicondyle of humerus.	Origin	From Ulna.
Insertion	Middle of Radius.	Insertion	Base of phalynx II of thumb.
Action	Pronates and flexes forearm.	Action	Abducts thumb.
Name	**Flexor Carpi Ulnaris**	Name	**Abductor Pollicis Longus**
Origin	Medial epincondyle of humerus.	Origin	From radius and ulna.
Insertion	Pisiform bone of wrist.	Insertion	Base of metacarpal I.
Action	Flexes forearm and hand.	Action	Abducts Thumb.
Name	**Extensor Pollicis Brevis**		
Origin	From radius.		
Insertion	Base of phalanx I of thumb.		
Action	Abducts thumb.		

Hand — Musculature

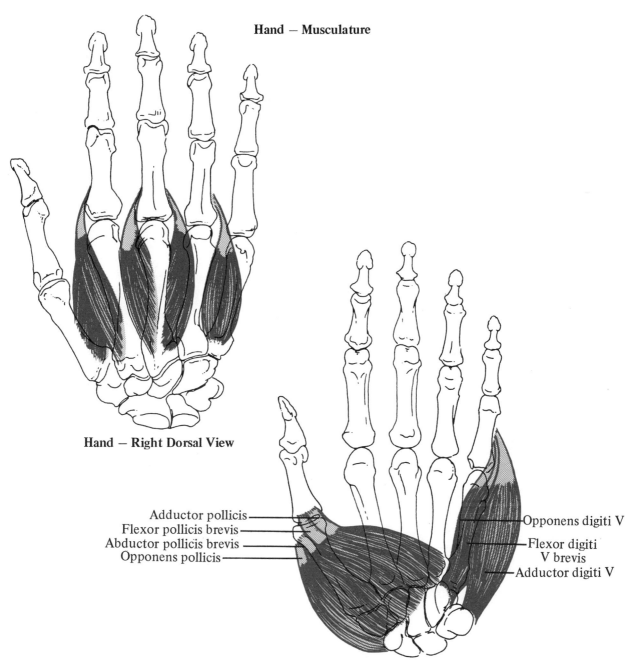

Hand — Right Dorsal View

Adductor pollicis
Flexor pollicis brevis
Abductor pollicis brevis
Opponens pollicis

Opponens digiti V
Flexor digiti V brevis
Adductor digiti V

Hand — Left Palmar View

Name	Action
Dorsal Interossei	Abduct fingers
Thumb Group	
Abductor Pollicis Brevis	Abducts thumb
Adductor Pollicis	
Oblique Head	Adducts thumb
Transverse Head	
Flexor Pollicis Brevis	Flexes thumb
Opponens Pollicis	Adducts, flexes and rotates thumbs
Little Finger Group	
Abductor Digiti V	Abducts little finger
Flexor Digiti V Brevis	Flexes little finger
Opponens Digiti V	Opposes little finger to thumb

Arm — Complete Musculature

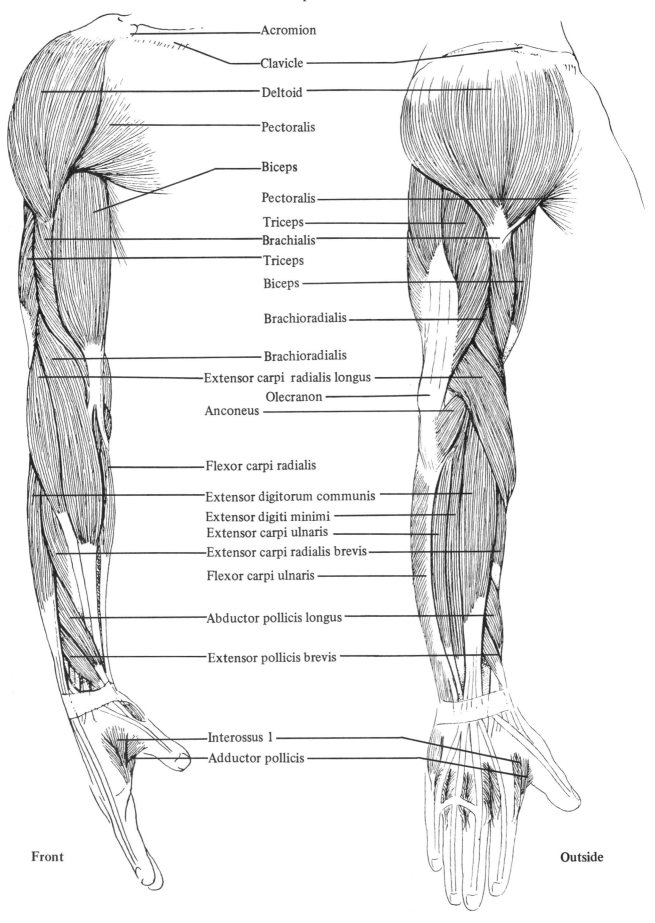

Acromion

Clavicle

Deltoid

Pectoralis

Biceps

Pectoralis

Triceps

Brachialis

Triceps

Biceps

Brachioradialis

Brachioradialis

Extensor carpi radialis longus

Olecranon

Anconeus

Flexor carpi radialis

Extensor digitorum communis

Extensor digiti minimi

Extensor carpi ulnaris

Extensor carpi radialis brevis

Flexor carpi ulnaris

Abductor pollicis longus

Extensor pollicis brevis

Interossus 1

Adductor pollicis

Front

Outside

44

Arm — Complete Musculature

Back

Inside

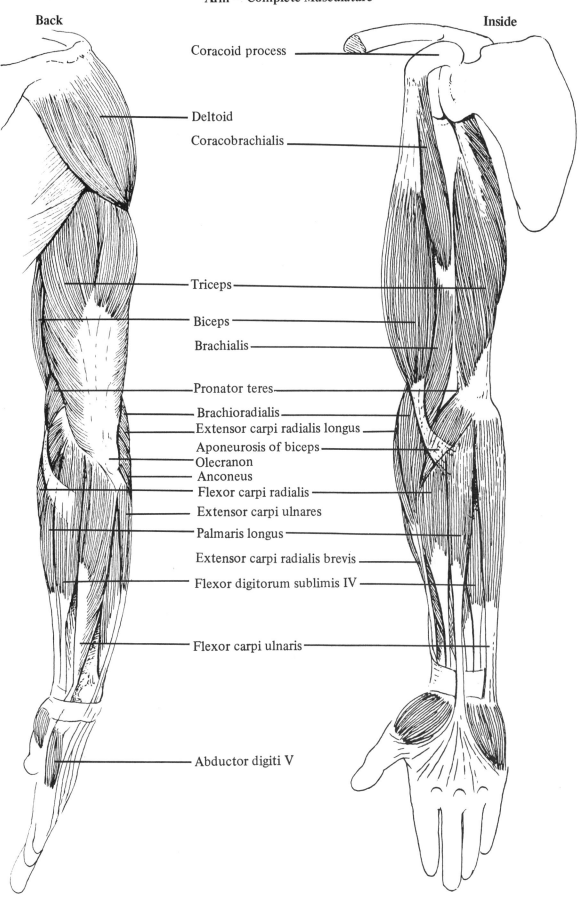

Coracoid process

Deltoid

Coracobrachialis

Triceps

Biceps

Brachialis

Pronator teres

Brachioradialis

Extensor carpi radialis longus

Aponeurosis of biceps

Olecranon

Anconeus

Flexor carpi radialis

Extensor carpi ulnares

Palmaris longus

Extensor carpi radialis brevis

Flexor digitorum sublimis IV

Flexor carpi ulnaris

Abductor digiti V

Leg – Musculature

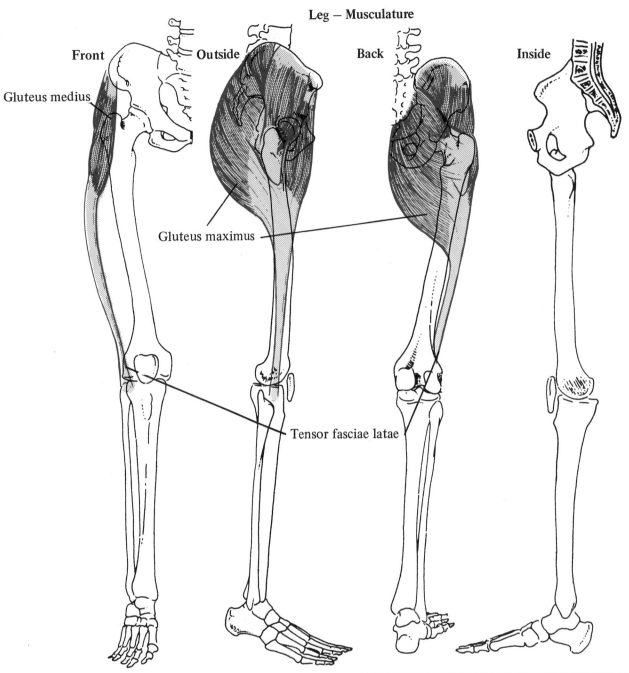

Front

Gluteus medius

Outside

Back

Inside

Gluteus maximus

Tensor fasciae latae

Name	**Gluteus Maximus**
Origin	Lateral surface of ilium, sacrum and coccyx.
Insertion	Posterior surface of femur and into ilio-tibial band.
Action	Extends thigh.
Name	**Gluteus Medius**
Origin	Lateral surface of ilium and iliac crest.
Insertion	Great trochanter of femur.
Action	Abducts thigh.
Name	**Tensor Fasciae Latae**
Origin	Front upper iliac spine.
Insertion	Into ilio-tibial band.
Action	Flexes, abducts and rotates thigh inwardly.

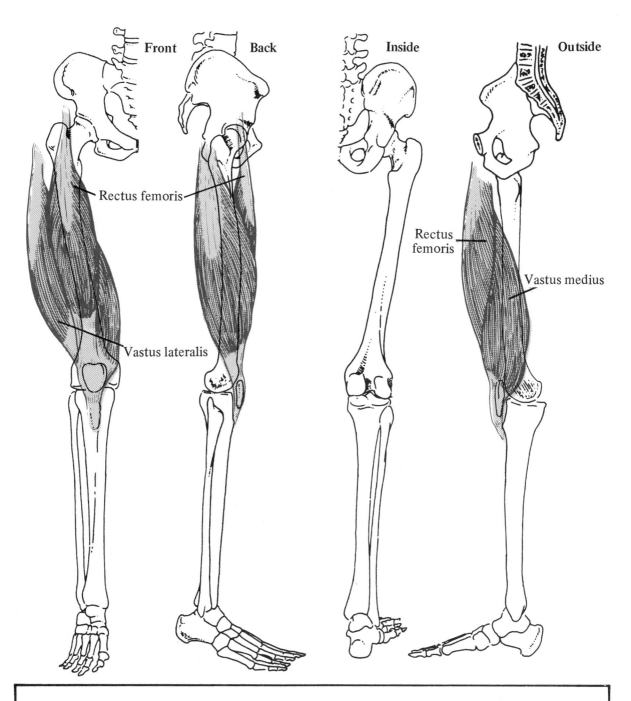

Front Back Inside Outside

Rectus femoris

Rectus femoris

Vastus medius

Vastus lateralis

Name	**Quadriceps Femoris** *(Composed of 4 muscles of which the following 3 appear on surface)*
	A. Rectus Femoris
Origin	Anterior — Inferior iliac spine.
	B. Vastus Lateralis
Origin	Great trochanter and linea aspera of femur.
	C. Vastus Medialis
Origin	Linea aspera
Insertion	*For all three* — Through a common tendon into the front tibial tuberosity. The patella bone lies inside this tendon.
Action	*For all three* — Extend the leg.

47

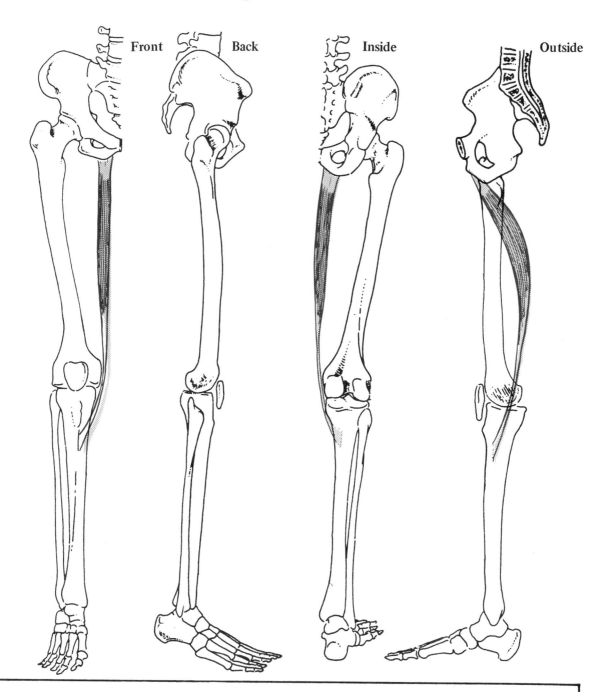

Front   Back   Inside   Outside

Name	Gracilis
Origin	Pubic symphysis.
Insertion	Tuberosity of tibia.
Action	Adducts and flexes thigh, flexes leg and rotates inwardly.

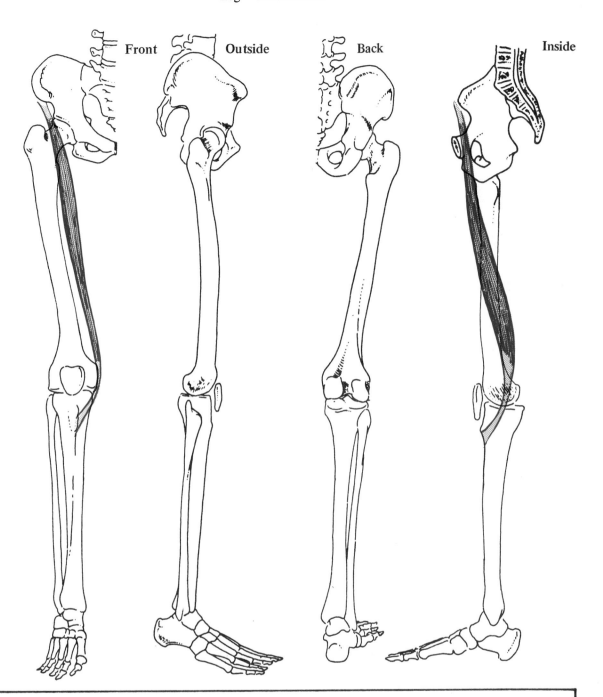

Front Outside Back Inside

Name	**Sartorius**
Origin	Front upper iliac spine.
Insertion	Behind tuberosity of tibia.
Action	Flexes, abducts and rotates thigh outwardly; with knee flexed, rotates leg inwardly.

Leg – Musculature

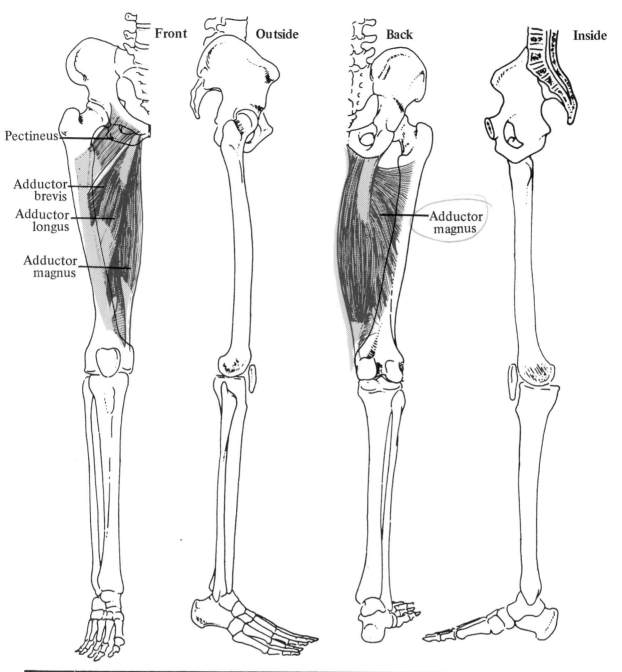

Front Outside Back Inside

Pectineus

Adductor brevis

Adductor longus

Adductor magnus

Adductor magnus

Name	Pectineus
Origin	Pubic crest.
Insertion	Behind small trochanter of femur.
Action	Flexes and adducts thigh.

Name	Adductor Magnus
Origin	Lower ramus of pubic bone and ramus of ischium
Insertion	Lower section of linea aspera of femur.
Action	Adducts thigh.

Name	Adductor Longus
Origin	Upper ramus of pubic bone.
Insertion	Middle of linea aspera of femur.
Action	Adducts, flexes thigh.

Leg – Musculature

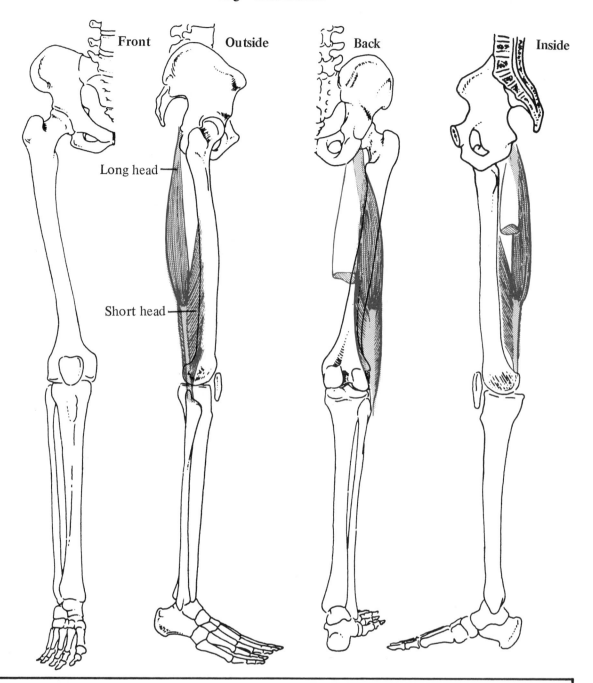

Front   Outside   Back   Inside

Long head

Short head

Name	**Biceps Femoris**
Origin	a) Longhead-Ischial tuberosity.
Origin	b) Shorthead-Linea aspera.
Insertion	Head of fibula.
Action	Flexes leg.

Leg — Musculature

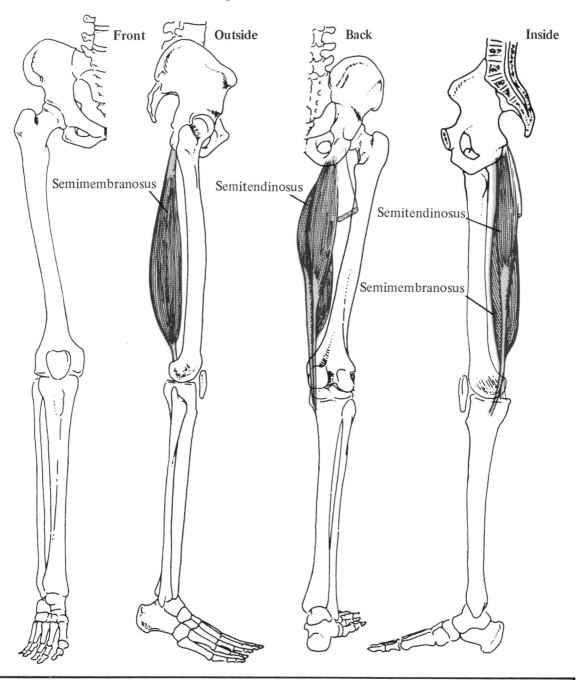

Front **Outside** **Back** **Inside**

Semimembranosus

Semitendinosus

Semitendinosus

Semimembranosus

Name	Semitendinosus
Origin	Ischial tuberosity
Insertion	Below medial condyle of tibia.
Action	Flexes leg.

Name	Semimembranosus
Origin	Ischial tuberosity
Insertion	Medial condyle of tibia.
Action	Flexes leg.

Leg – Musculature

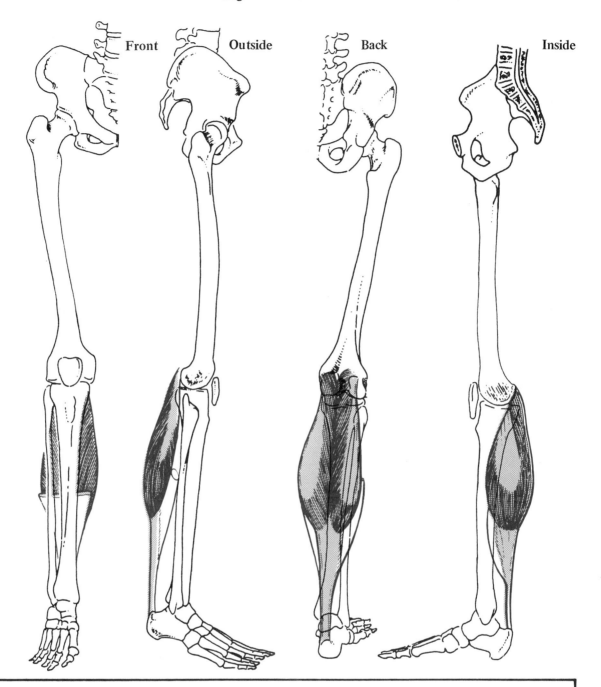

Front   Outside   Back   Inside

Name	**Gastrocnemius**
Origin	Lateral condyle of femur.
Insertion	Into calcaneus bone through the Achilles tendon.
Action	Extends foot. Flexes leg.

Leg – Musculature

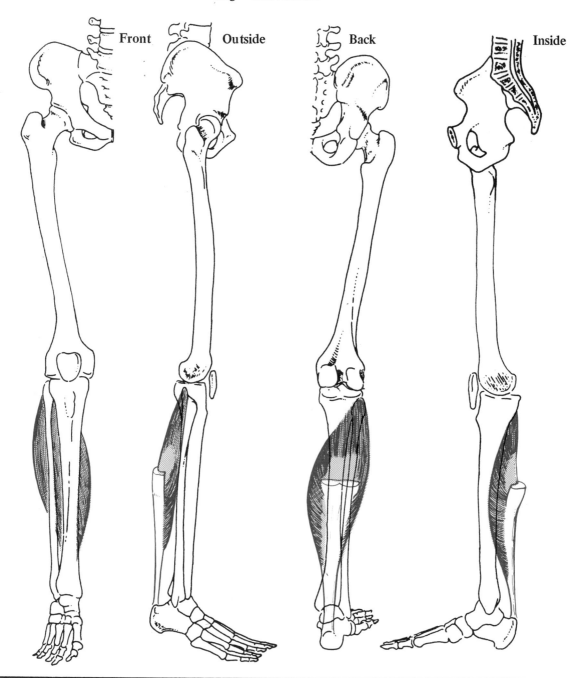

Front   Outside   Back   Inside

Name	Soleus
Origin	Fibula head – back surface of fibula and tibia.
Insertion	Into calcaneus bone through the Achilles tendon.
Action	Extends foot.

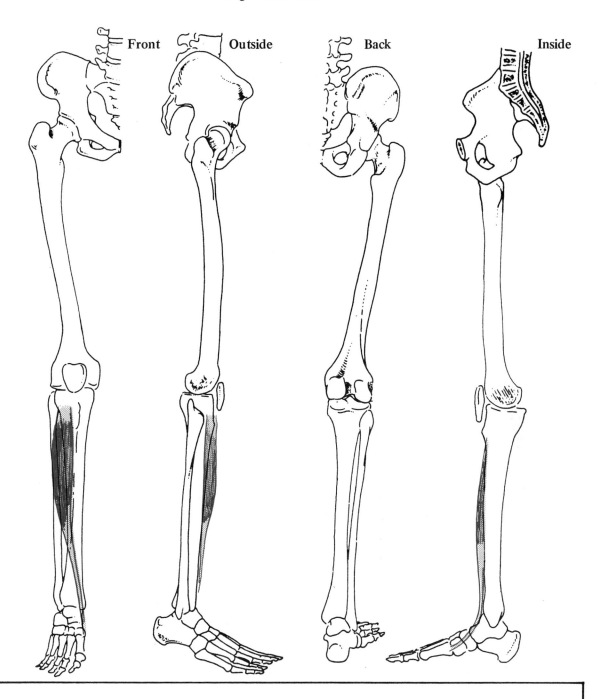

Front   Outside   Back   Inside

Name	**Tibialis Anterior**
Origin	Lateral condyle and lateral surface of tibia.
Insertion	1st cuneiform bone of ankle and metatarsal of great toe.
Action	Flexes foot – elevates inner border of foot.

55

Leg – Musculature

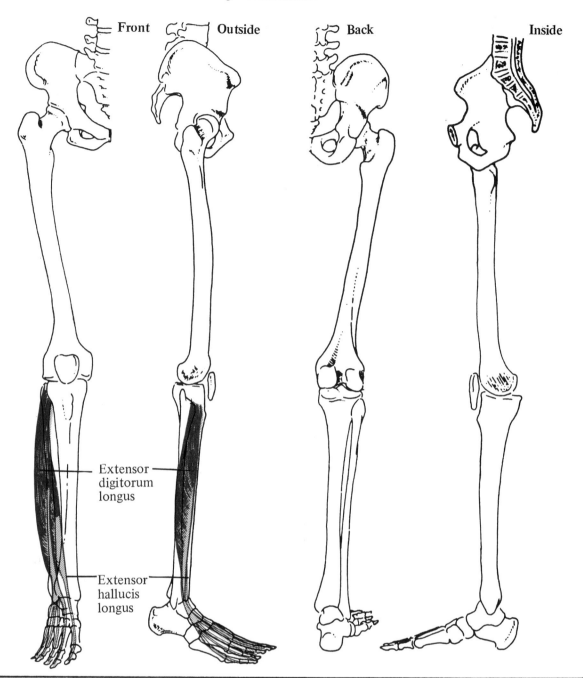

Front **Outside** **Back** **Inside**

Extensor
digitorum
longus

Extensor
hallucis
longus

Name	**Extensor Digitorum Longus**
Origin	Lateral condyle of tibia and front edge of fibula.
Insertion	By 4 tendons to phalanges of 2nd to 4th toes.
Action	Extends toes II to IV.

Name	**Extensor Hallucis Longus**
Origin	Medial surface of fibula.
Insertion	Base of 2nd phalanx of big toe.
Action	Extends big toe.

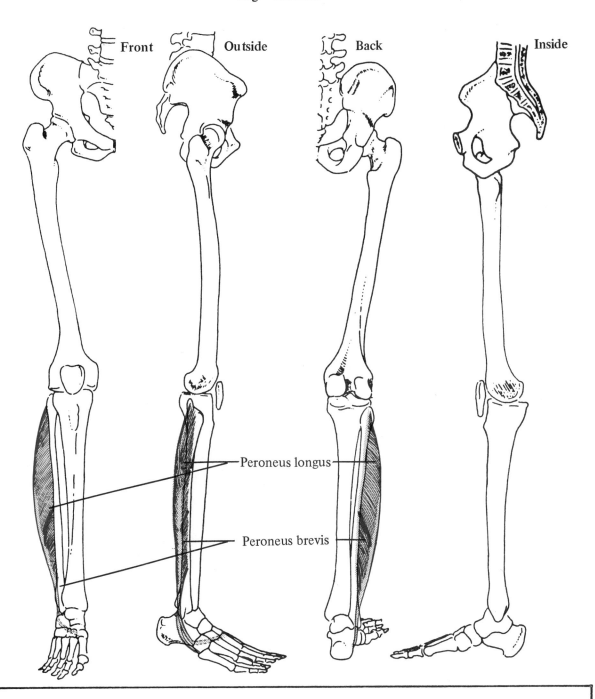

Front   Outside   Back   Inside

Peroneus longus

Peroneus brevis

Name	**Peroneus Longus**
Origin	Head and upper lateral surface of fibula.
Insertion	1st cuneiform and 1st metatarsal bone and to sole of foot.
Action	Flexes and raises lateral edge of foot.
Name	**Peroneus Brevis**
Origin	Lower lateral half of fibula.
Insertion	Tuberosity of 5th metatarsal bone.
Action	Flexes and raises lateral edge of foot.

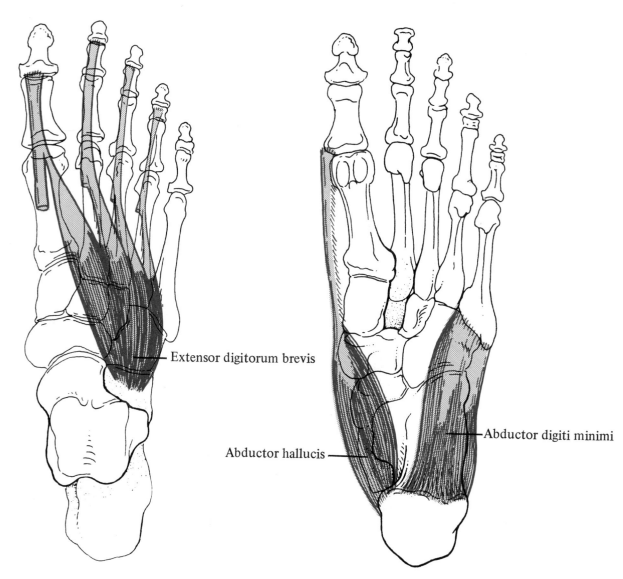

Extensor digitorum brevis

Abductor hallucis —

—Abductor digiti minimi

Right — Dorsal View   **Left — Plantar View**

Name	**Abductor Hallucis**
Origin	Tuberosity of calcaneus, etc.
Insertion	Base of 1st phalanx of big toe.
Action	Abducts big toe.
Name	**Abductor Digiti Minimi**
Origin	Lateral and underside of calcaneus.
Insertion	Base of proximal phalanx of little toe.
Action	Abducts little toe.
Name	**Extensor Digitorum Brevis**
Origin	Upper surface of calcaneus.
Insertion	By 4 tendons to 2nd phalanges of toes II to IV.
Action	Extension of toes.

Leg – Complete Musculature

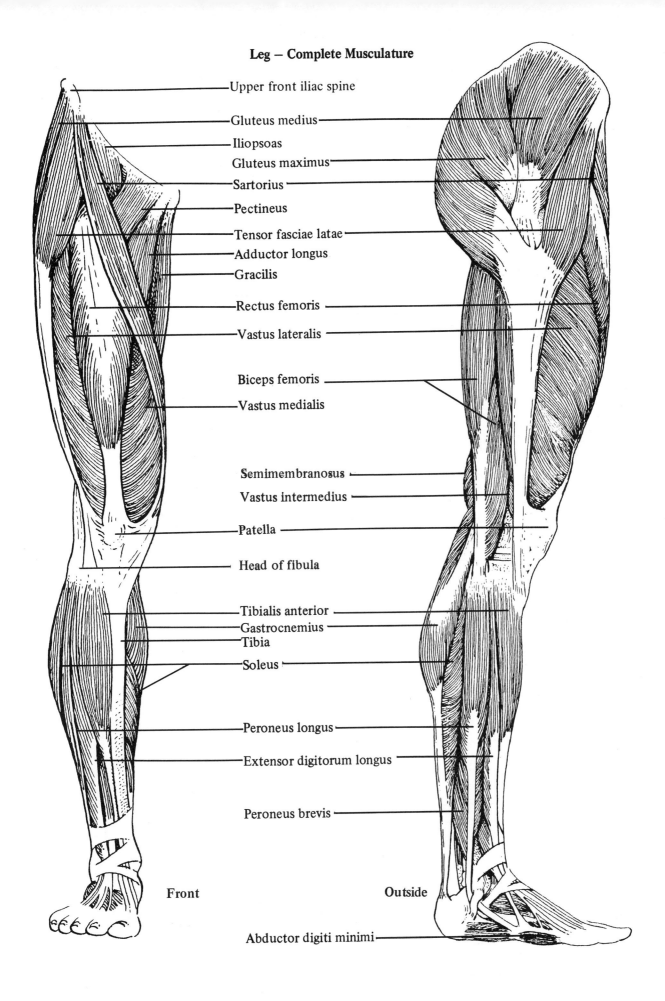

Upper front iliac spine

Gluteus medius

Iliopsoas

Gluteus maximus

Sartorius

Pectineus

Tensor fasciae latae

Adductor longus

Gracilis

Rectus femoris

Vastus lateralis

Biceps femoris

Vastus medialis

Semimembranosus

Vastus intermedius

Patella

Head of fibula

Tibialis anterior

Gastrocnemius

Tibia

Soleus

Peroneus longus

Extensor digitorum longus

Peroneus brevis

Front

Outside

Abductor digiti minimi

59

Leg — Complete Musculature

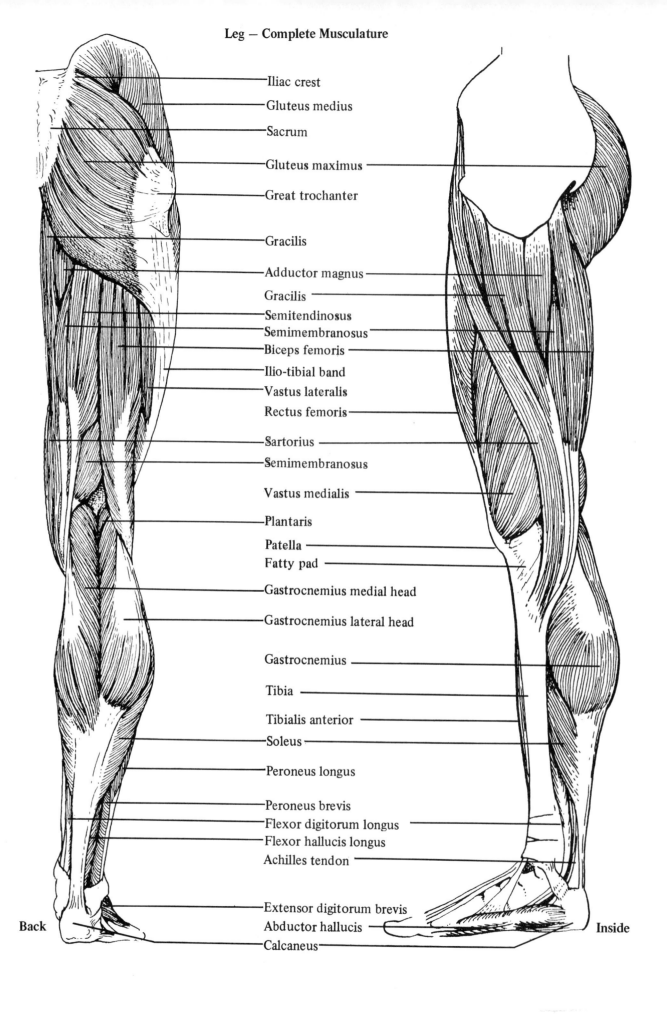

Iliac crest

Gluteus medius

Sacrum

Gluteus maximus

Great trochanter

Gracilis

Adductor magnus

Gracilis

Semitendinosus

Semimembranosus

Biceps femoris

Ilio-tibial band

Vastus lateralis

Rectus femoris

Sartorius

Semimembranosus

Vastus medialis

Plantaris

Patella

Fatty pad

Gastrocnemius medial head

Gastrocnemius lateral head

Gastrocnemius

Tibia

Tibialis anterior

Soleus

Peroneus longus

Peroneus brevis

Flexor digitorum longus

Flexor hallucis longus

Achilles tendon

Extensor digitorum brevis

Abductor hallucis

Calcaneus

Back

Inside

60

FAT IN RELATION TO FORM

We are concerned here with the fatty accumulations that lie between the fascia covering muscles and the skin. In these places fat tends to fill in the grooves between muscles and hide their shape. In the same fashion it rounds off contours and smooths the shapes of forms. It is almost impossible to define the proportion of fat or how it determines the form of a figure. There are thin, medium and fat figures. The fat on two figures can vary a great deal. What can be said, in general, is that the location of fat is usually confined to the areas indicated on plates

The female figure has a greater proportion of fat than the male. In the areas of the flank, buttock, front and side of the thigh, and the upper back of the arm there is a much greater accumulation on the female than the male. In the front of the figure, there is a greater accumulation on the top half of the abdomen (rectus abdominus area) in the male and in the bottom half in the female. The female figure also has a larger accumulation in the pre-pubic area and in the top back of the shoulder (trapezius area). These areas are illustrated showing both female and male figures on pages 62 and 63.

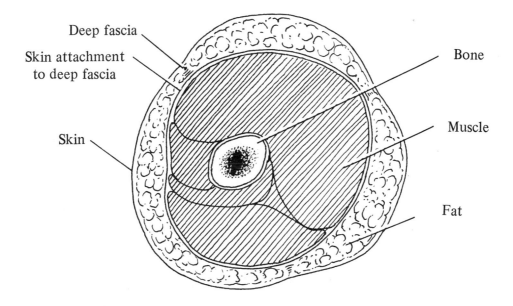

Deep fascia

Skin attachment
to deep fascia

Skin

Bone

Muscle

Fat

Fatty Tissue – Front

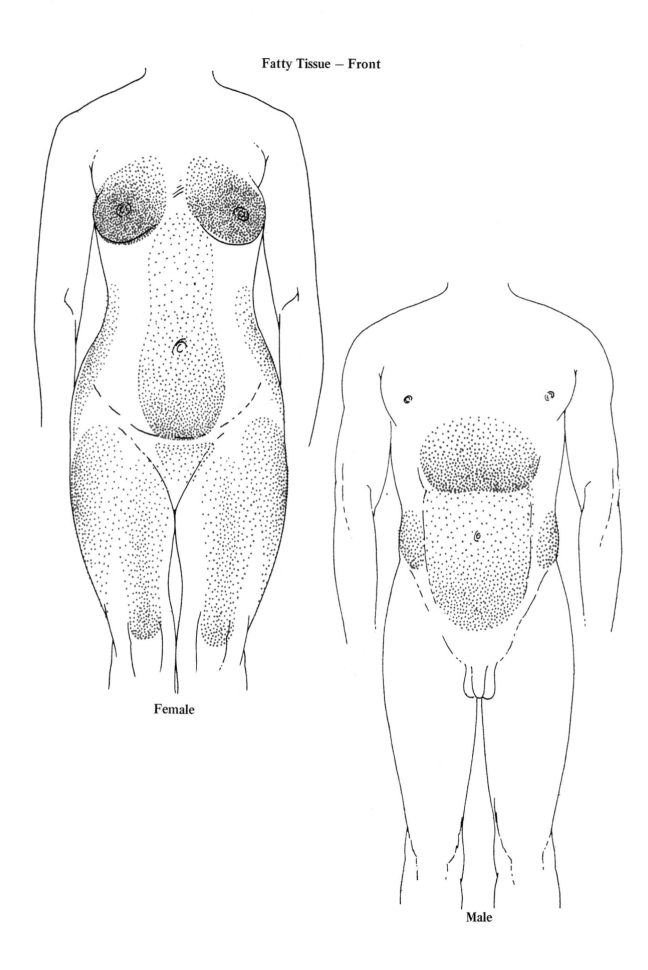

Female

Male

62

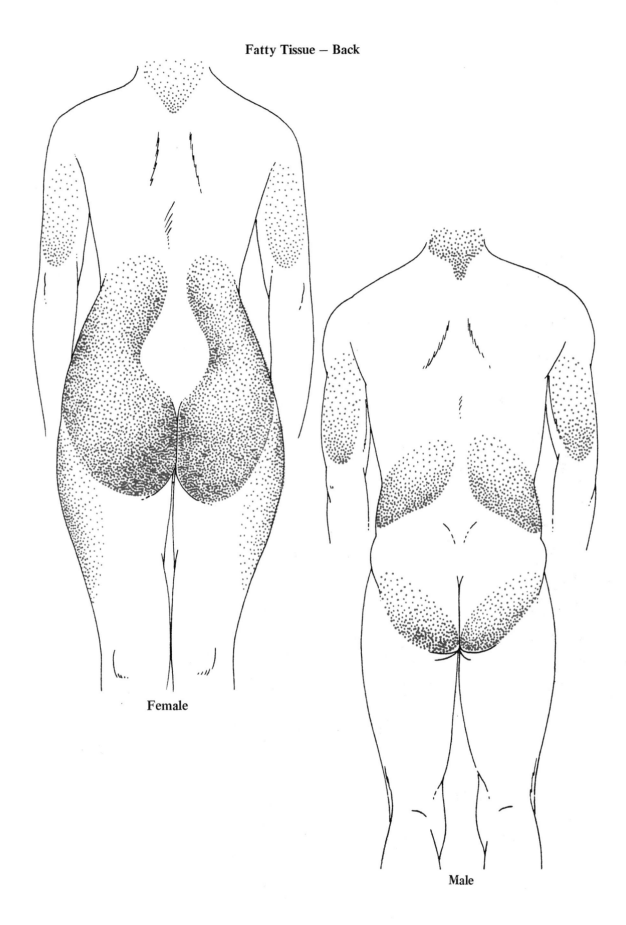

Female

Male

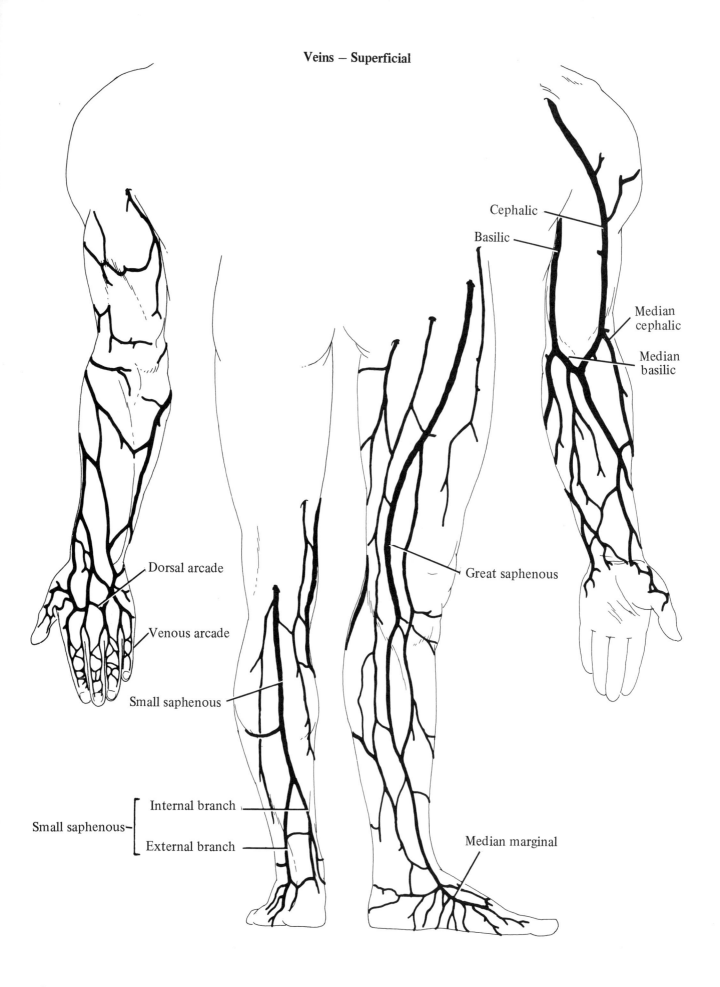

Cephalic

Basilic

Median cephalic

Median basilic

Dorsal arcade

Venous arcade

Great saphenous

Small saphenous

Small saphenous

Internal branch

External branch

Median marginal

WORKBOOK

Assignment Check List

In the spaces below write in the name and page number of work plates assigned by instructor.

Plate Name	Page	Date Due		Plate Name	Page	Date Due

Skeleton — Front

67

_____

_____

_____

_____

_____

_____

Humerus ——————————

_____

_____

_____

_____

_____

_____

_____

_____

_____

_____

_____

_____

_____

_____

Finish skeleton in red. Print names of bones at left in indicated spaces. Draw horizontal lines in BLACK to bones.

NAME_____ SECTION_____ DATE_____

Humerus ————————————————————————

Finish skeleton in red. Print names of bones at left in indicated spaces. Draw horizontal lines in BLACK to bones.

NAME_____ SECTION_____ DATE_____

Skeleton – Back

Humerus

(blank labeling lines at left)

Finish skeleton in red. Print names of bones at left in indicated spaces. Draw horizontal lines in BLACK to bones.

NAME_____ SECTION_____ DATE_____

71

_____
_____
_____
_____
_____
_____
_____
_____
_____
_____
_____
_____
_____
_____
_____
_____
_____
_____
_____
_____

Finish bones of head in red. Print names of bones at left. Draw horizontal lines in BLACK to bones.

_NAME_____ _SECTION_____ _DATE_____

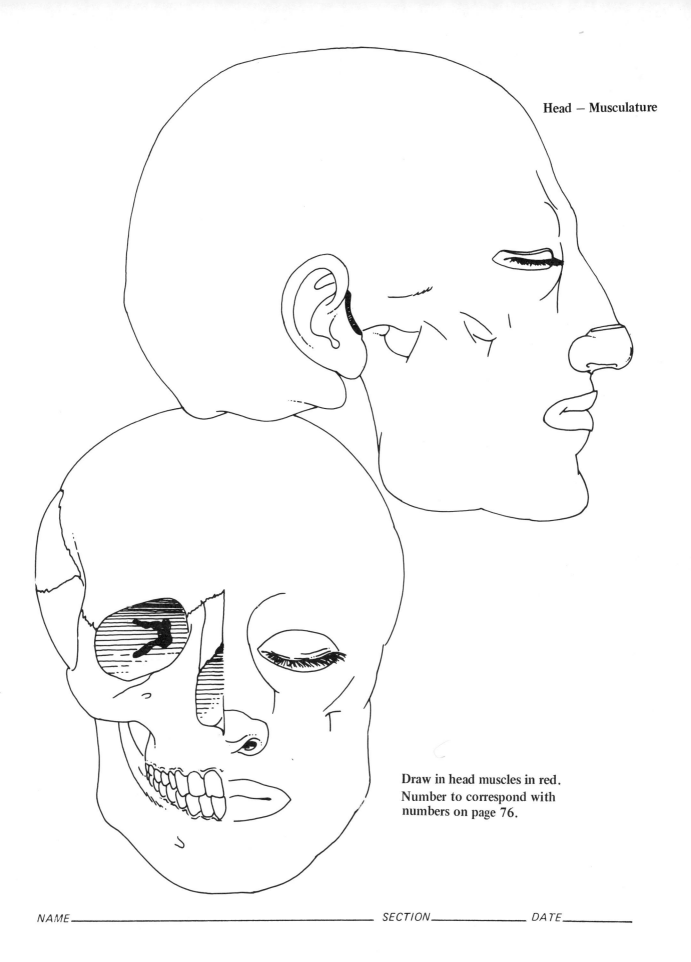

Draw in head muscles in red.
Number to correspond with
numbers on page 76.

NAME _____ SECTION _____ DATE _____

HEAD — MUSCULATURE

Fill in the action caused by the corresponding muscle.

Name   **Action**

1. Buccinator   _____
2. Digastric   _____
3. Frontalis   _____
4. Masseter   _____
5. Mentalis   _____
6. Nasalis   _____
7. Orbicularis Oculi   _____
8. Orbicularis Oris   _____
9. Procerus   _____
10. Quadratus Labii Inferioris   _____
11. Quadratus Labii Superioris   _____
      a) Infraorbital Head   _____
      b) Angular Head   _____
      c) Zygomaticus Minor   _____
12. Risorius   _____
13. Temporalis   _____
14. Triangularis   _____
15. Zygomaticus Major   _____

HEAD MUSCLES

Name	**Frontalis**	Name	**Orbicularis Oris**
Origin	_____	Origin	_____
Insertion	_____	Insertion	_____
Action	_____	Action	_____

Name	**Masseter**	Name	**Temporalis**
Origin	_____	Origin	_____
Insertion	_____	Insertion	_____
Action	_____	Action	_____

Name	**Orbicularis Oculi**	Name	**Triangularis**
Origin	_____	Origin	_____
Insertion	_____	Insertion	_____
Action	_____	Action	_____

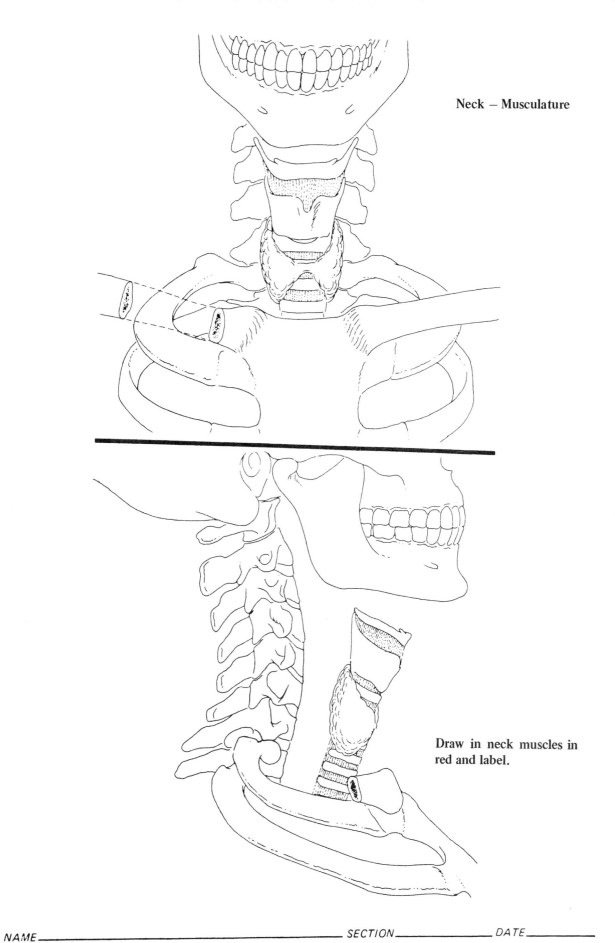

Neck — Musculature

Draw in neck muscles in red and label.

NECK — MUSCULATURE

Name   **Platysma**

Origin   _____

Insertion   _____

Action   _____

Name   **Digastric**

Origin   _____

Insertion   _____

Action   _____

Name   **Omohyoid**

Origin   _____

Insertion   _____

Action   _____

Name   **Sternohyoid**

Origin   _____

Insertion   _____

Action   _____

Name   **Sternothyroid**

Origin   _____

Insertion   _____

Action   _____

Name   **Thyrohyoid**

Origin   _____

Insertion   _____

Action   _____

Name   **Scalenus** *(Anterior, Medius, Posterior)*

Origin   _____

Insertion   _____

Action   _____

Torso — Musculature

Front   Side   Back

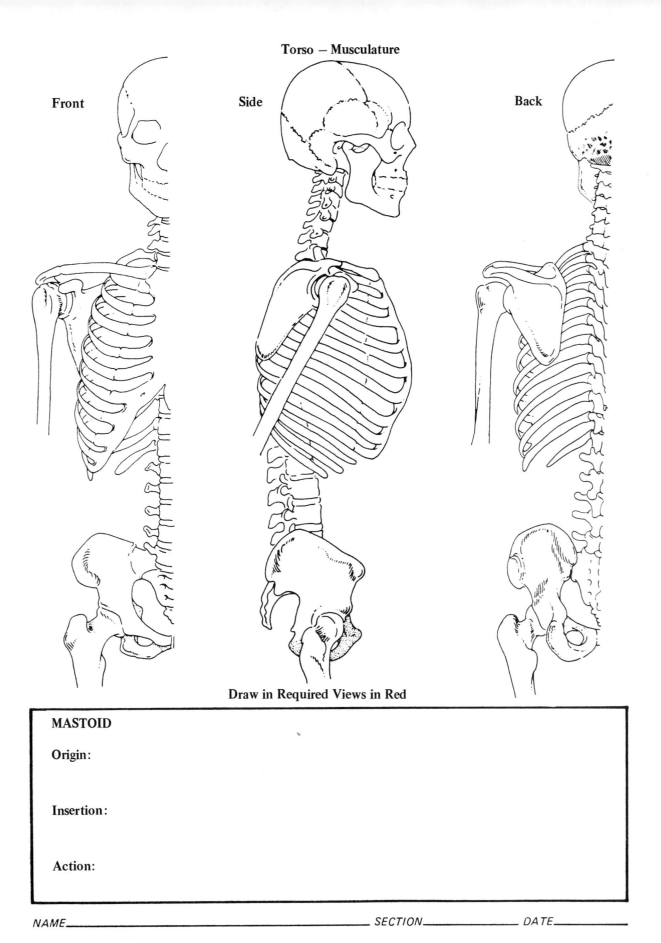

Draw in Required Views in Red

MASTOID

Origin:

Insertion:

Action:

*NAME*_____ *SECTION*_____ *DATE*_____

Torso — Musculature

Front   Side   Back

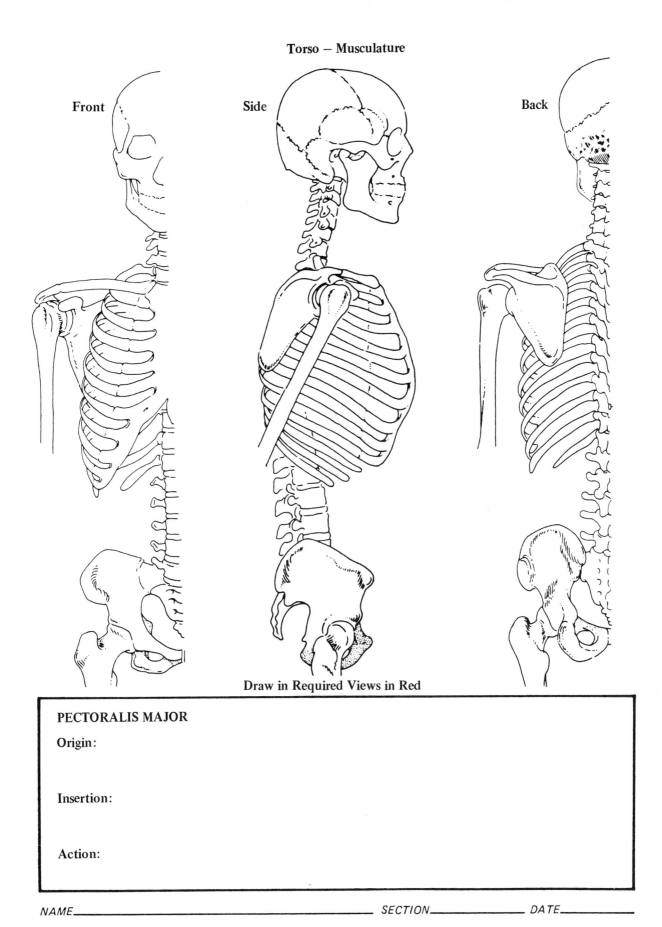

Draw in Required Views in Red

PECTORALIS MAJOR

Origin:

Insertion:

Action:

*NAME*_____ *SECTION*_____ *DATE*_____

81

Torso — Musculature

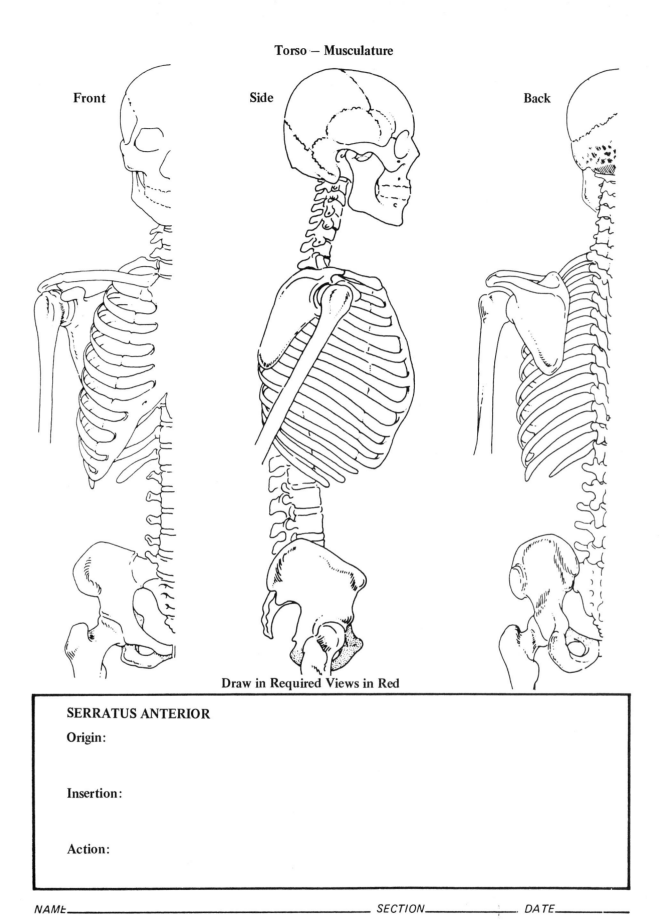

Front

Side

Back

Draw in Required Views in Red

SERRATUS ANTERIOR

Origin:

Insertion:

Action:

Torso — Musculature

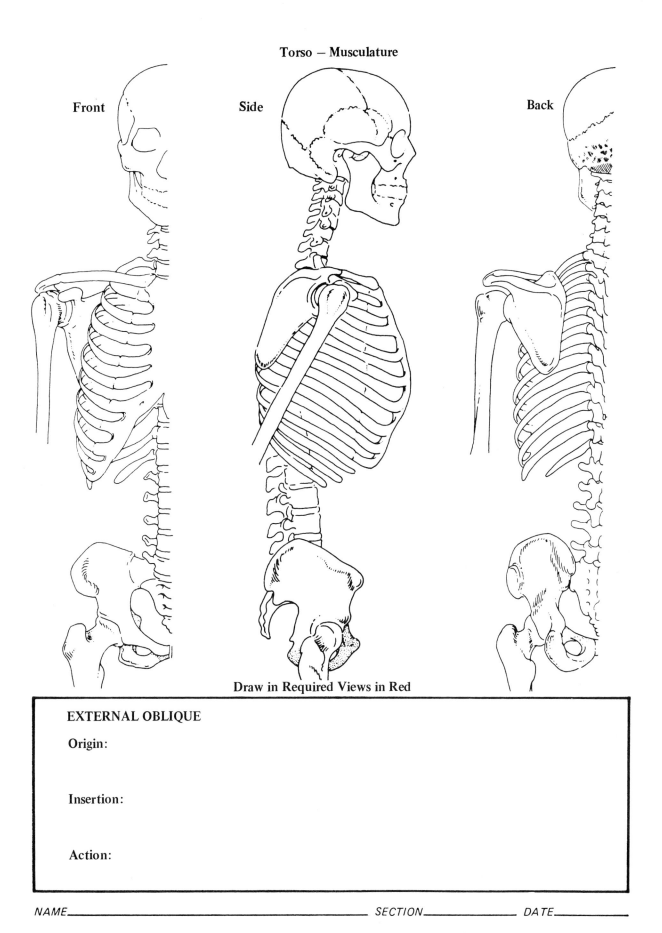

Front   Side   Back

Draw in Required Views in Red

EXTERNAL OBLIQUE

Origin:

Insertion:

Action:

*NAME*_____ *SECTION*_____ *DATE*_____

Torso — Musculature

Front   Side   Back

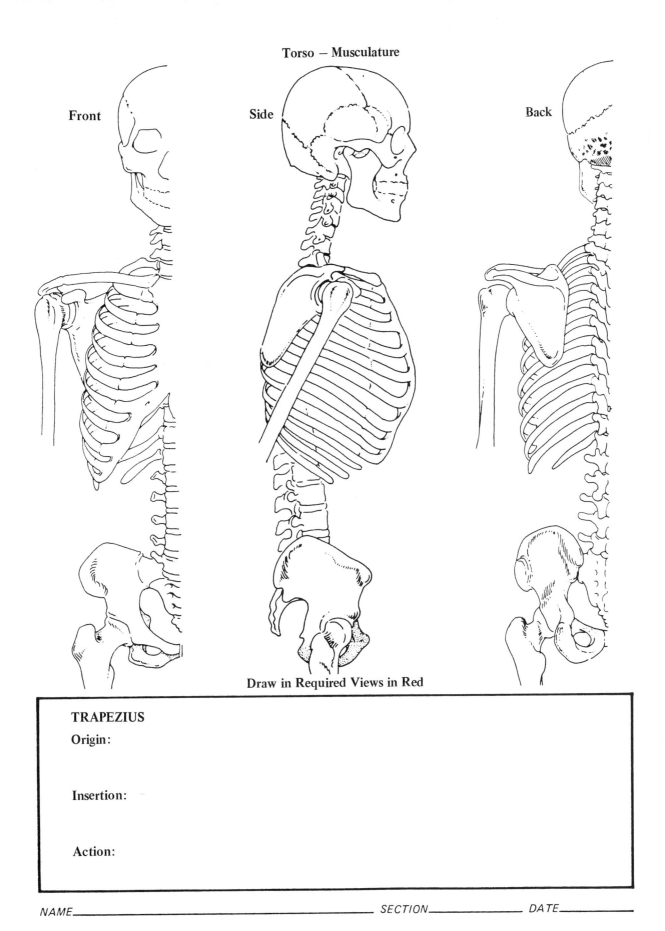

Draw in Required Views in Red

TRAPEZIUS

Origin:

Insertion:

Action:

*NAME*_____ *SECTION*_____ *DATE*_____

89

Torso — Musculature

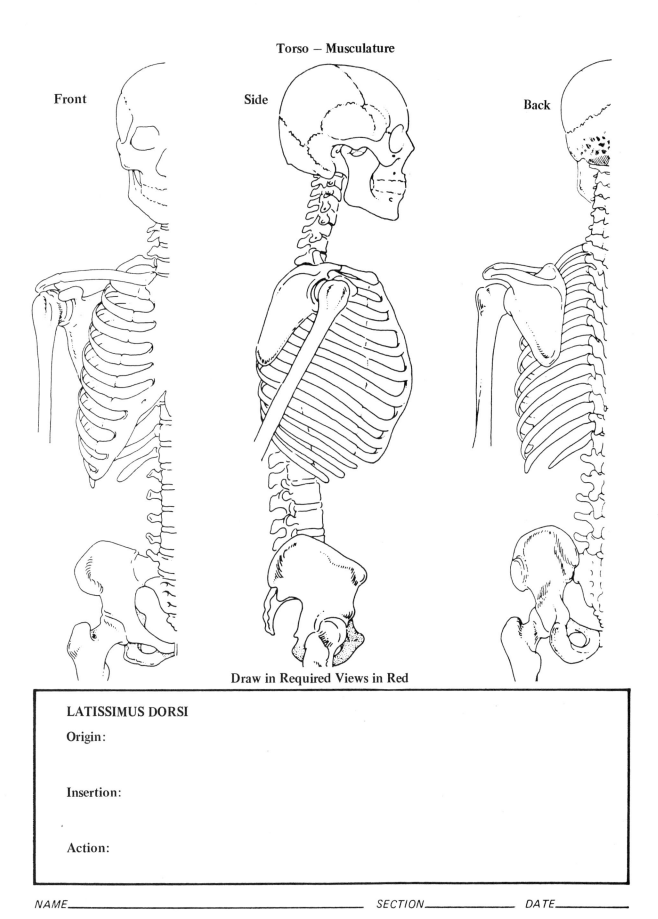

Front   Side   Back

Draw in Required Views in Red

LATISSIMUS DORSI

Origin:

Insertion:

Action:

NAME_____ SECTION_____ DATE_____

Torso — Musculature

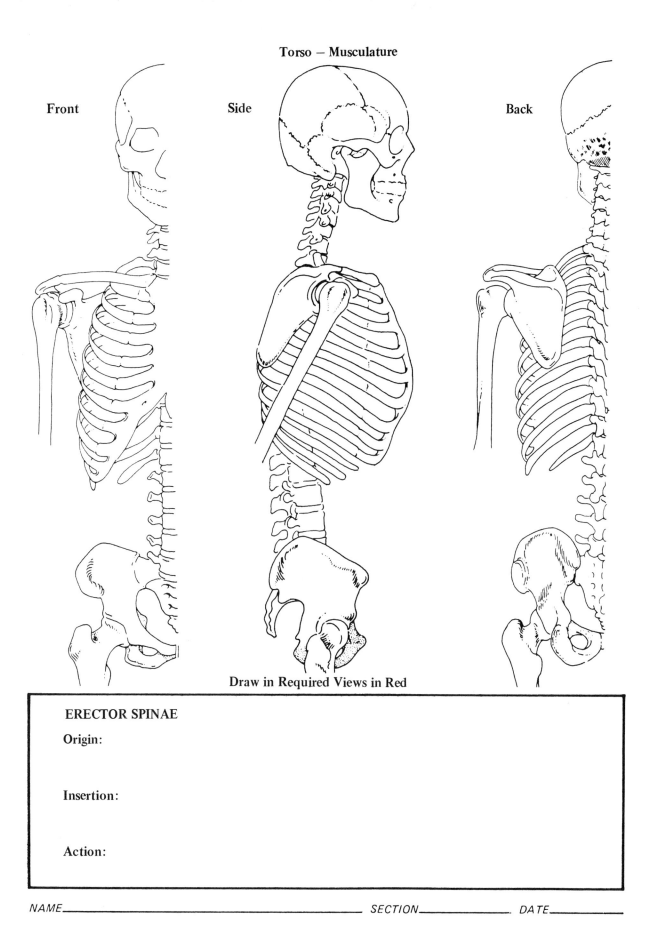

Front

Side

Back

Draw in Required Views in Red

ERECTOR SPINAE

Origin:

Insertion:

Action:

*NAME*_____ *SECTION*_____ *DATE*_____

Torso — Musculature

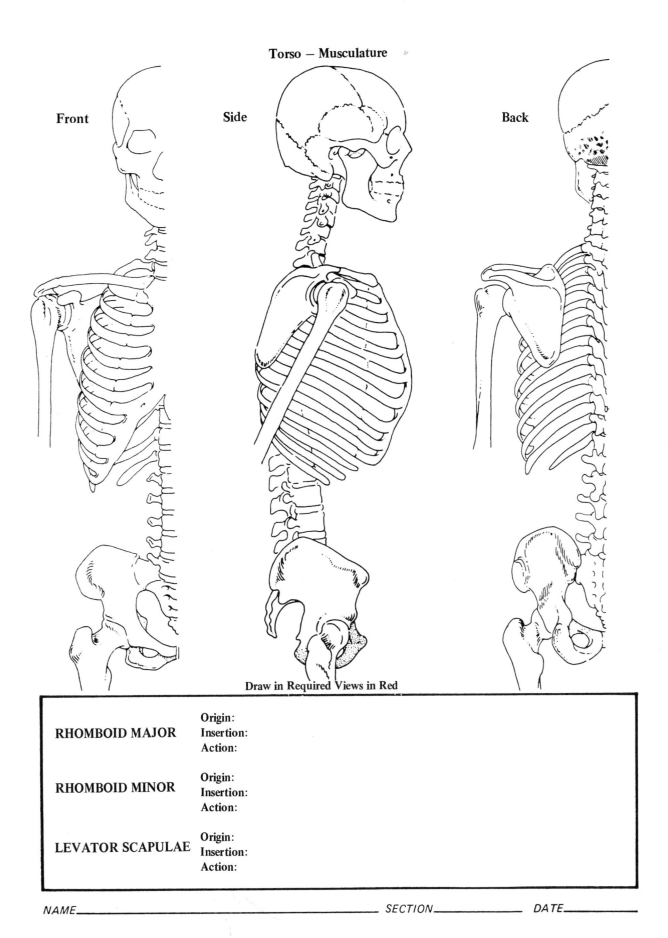

Front   Side   Back

Draw in Required Views in Red

RHOMBOID MAJOR	Origin: Insertion: Action:	
RHOMBOID MINOR	Origin: Insertion: Action:	
LEVATOR SCAPULAE	Origin: Insertion: Action:	

NAME_____ SECTION_____ DATE_____

Torso — Musculature

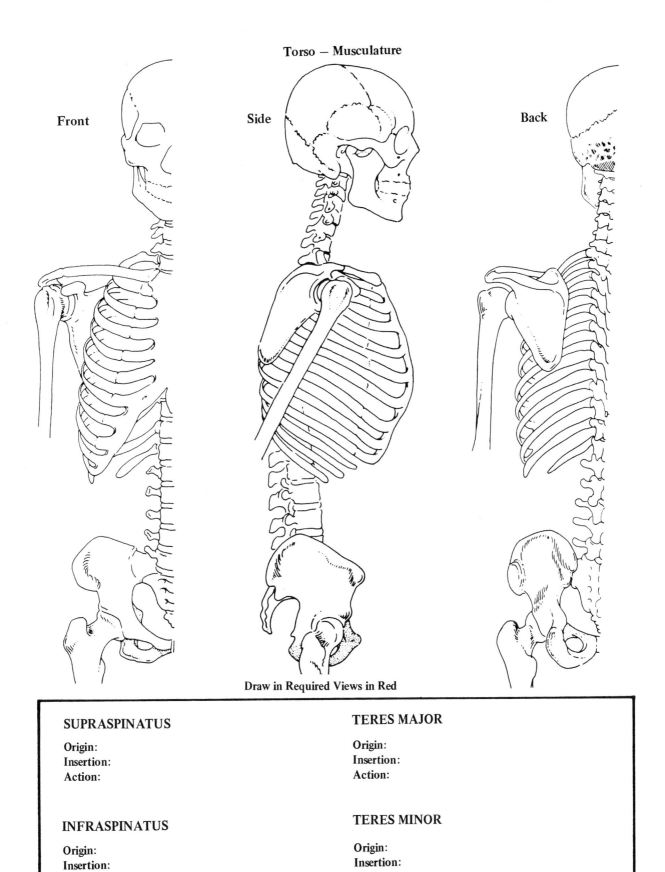

Front   Side   Back

Draw in Required Views in Red

SUPRASPINATUS

Origin:
Insertion:
Action:

TERES MAJOR

Origin:
Insertion:
Action:

INFRASPINATUS

Origin:
Insertion:
Action:

TERES MINOR

Origin:
Insertion:
Action:

NAME_____ SECTION_____ DATE_____

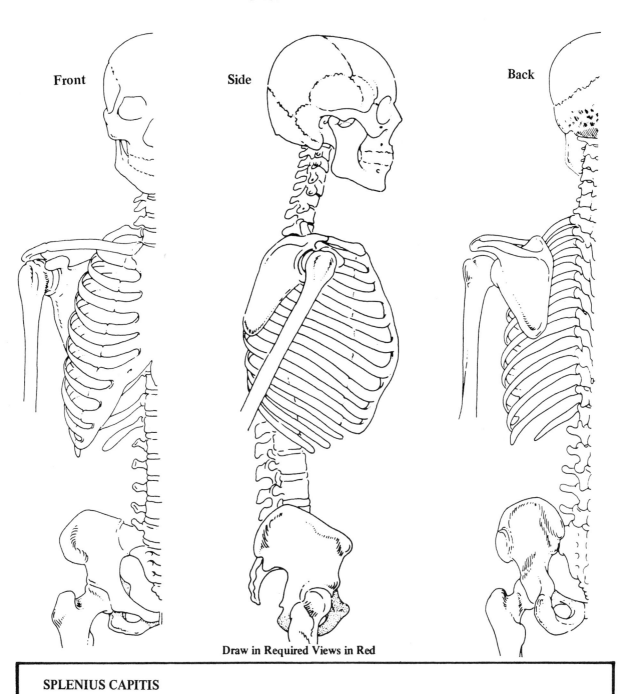

Front   Side   Back

Draw in Required Views in Red

SPLENIUS CAPITIS

Origin:
Insertion:
Action:

SPLENIUS CERVICIS

Origin:
Insertion:
Action:

*NAME*_____ *SECTION*_____ *DATE*_____

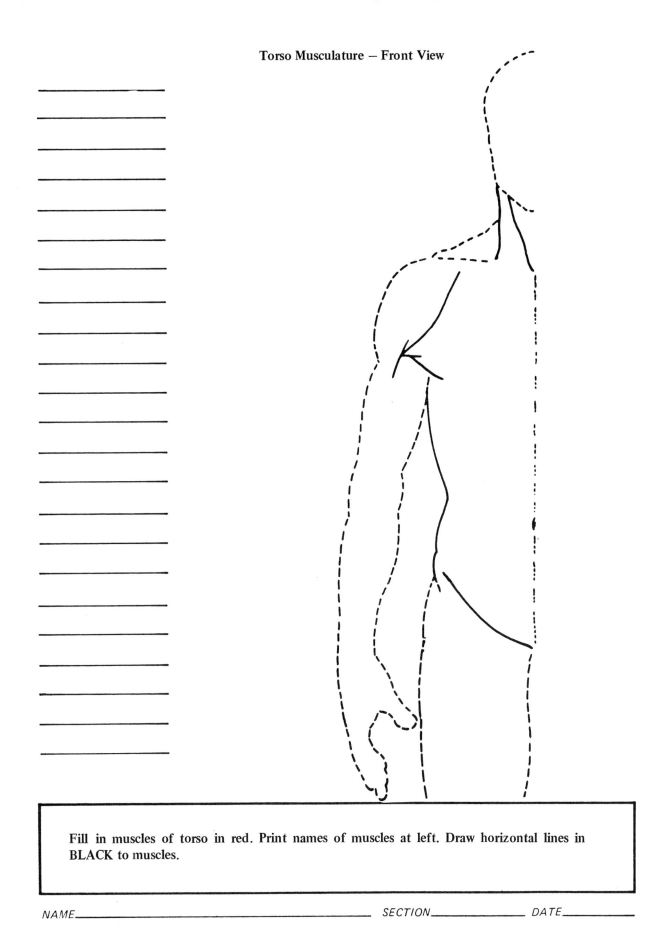

Fill in muscles of torso in red. Print names of muscles at left. Draw horizontal lines in BLACK to muscles.

*NAME*_____ *SECTION*_____ *DATE*_____

_____
_____
_____
_____
_____
_____
_____
_____
_____
_____
_____
_____
_____
_____
_____
_____
_____
_____

Fill in muscles of torso in red. Print names of muscles at left. Draw horizontal lines in BLACK to muscles.

NAME_____ SECTION_____ DATE_____

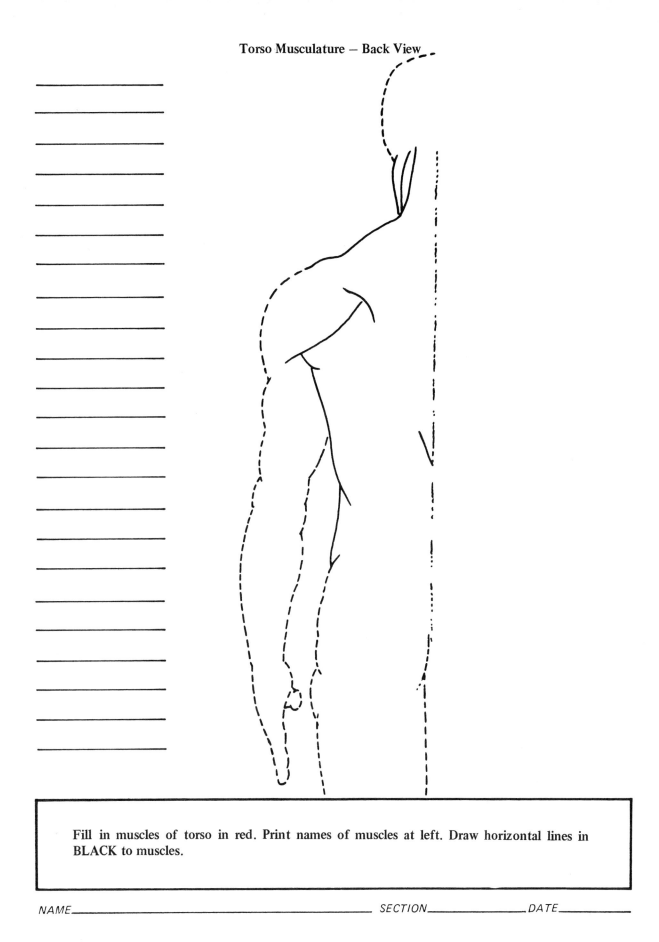

Fill in muscles of torso in red. Print names of muscles at left. Draw horizontal lines in BLACK to muscles.

NAME_____ SECTION_____ DATE_____

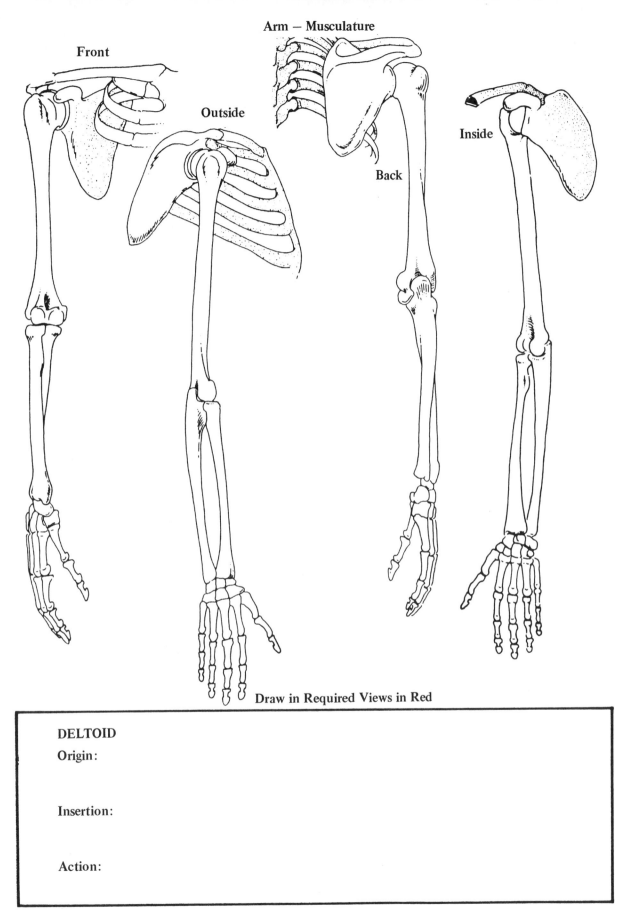

Arm – Musculature

Front

Outside

Back

Inside

Draw in Required Views in Red

DELTOID

Origin:

Insertion:

Action:

Arm – Musculature

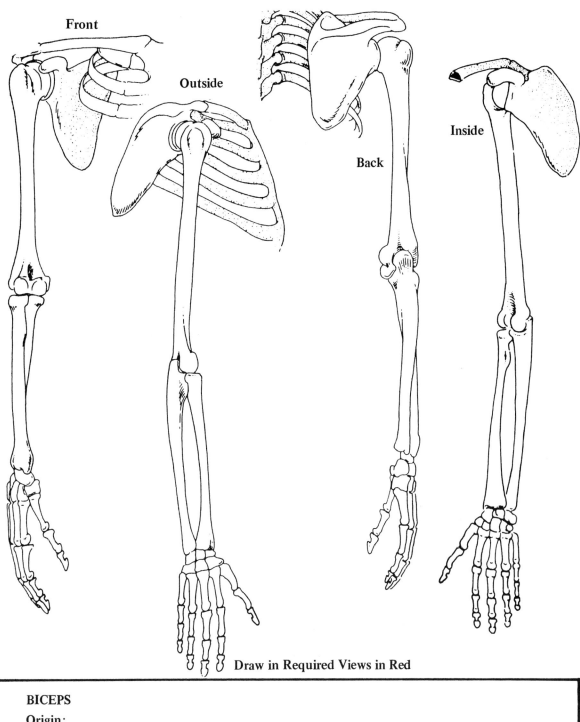

Front

Outside

Back

Inside

Draw in Required Views in Red

BICEPS
Origin:

Insertion:

Action:

*NAME*_____ *SECTION*_____ *DATE*_____

Arm — Musculature

Front

Outside

Back

Inside

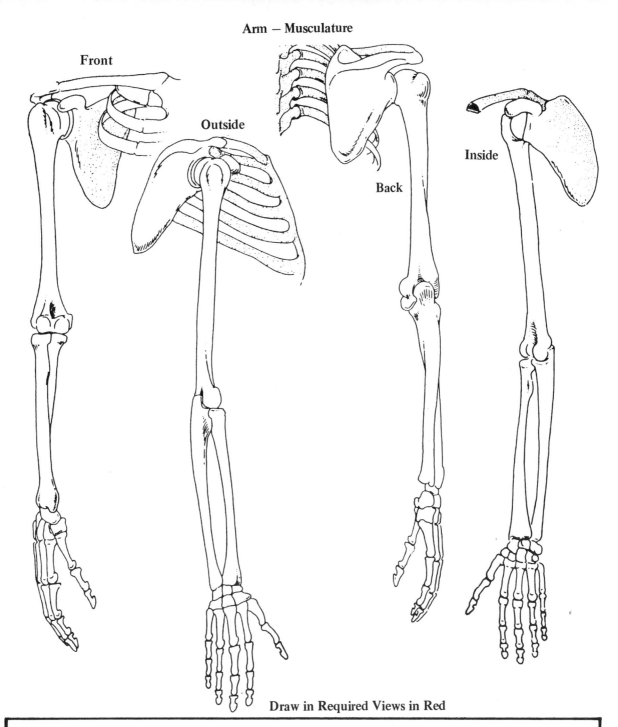

Draw in Required Views in Red

CORACOBRACHIAIS

Origin:
Insertion:
Action:

BRACHIALIS

Origin:
Insertion:
Action:

*NAME*_____ *SECTION*_____ *DATE*_____

Arm — Musculature

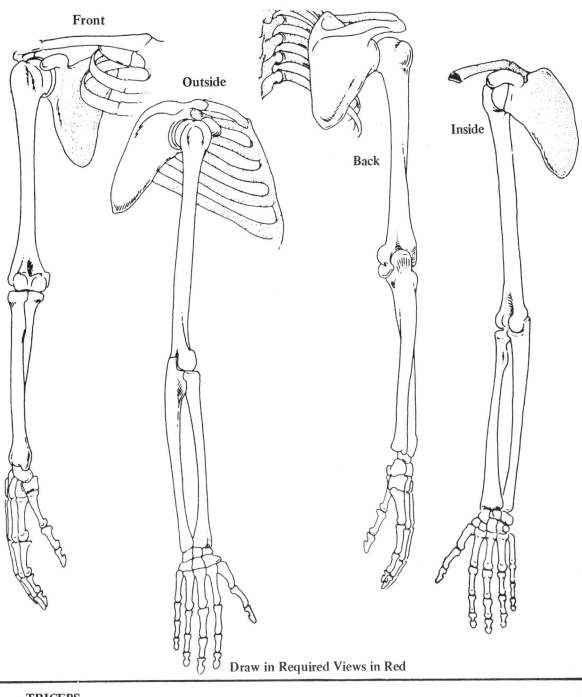

Front

Outside

Back

Inside

Draw in Required Views in Red

TRICEPS
Origin:

Insertion:

Action:

NAME_____ SECTION_____ DATE_____

Arm – Musculature

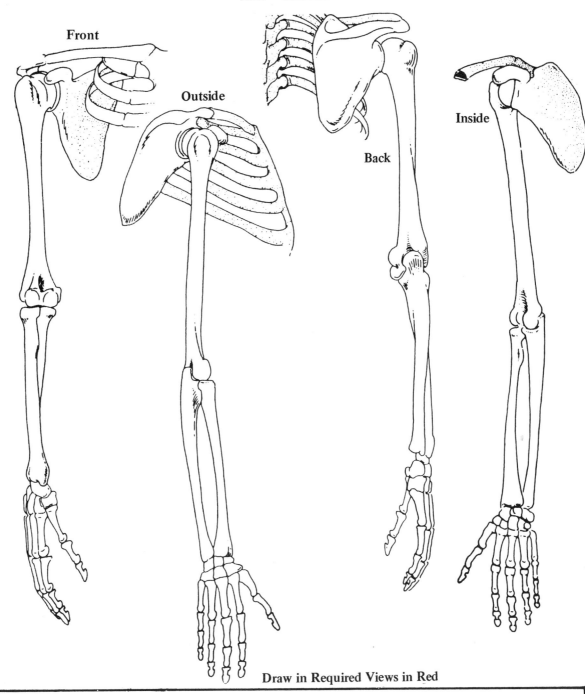

Front

Outside

Back

Inside

Draw in Required Views in Red

BRACHIORADIALIS

Origin:
Insertion:
Action:

EXTENSOR CARPI RADIALIS BREVIS

Origin:
Insertion:
Action:

EXTENSOR CARPI RADIALIS LONGUS

Origin:
Insertion:
Action:

NAME_____ SECTION_____ DATE_____

Arm – Musculature

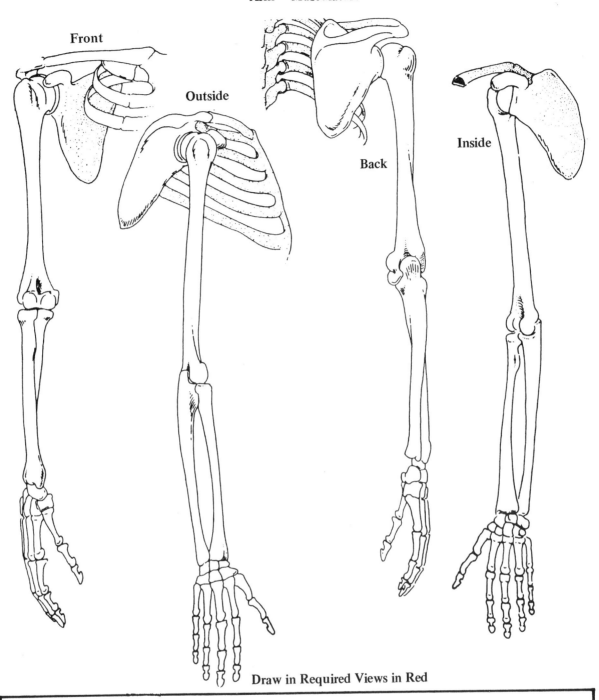

Front

Outside

Back

Inside

Draw in Required Views in Red

EXTENSOR CARPI ULNARIS	**EXTENSOR DIGITI V**
Origin:	Origin:
Insertion:	Insertion:
Action:	Action:
EXTENSOR DIGITORUM COMMUNIS	
Origin:	
Insertion:	
Action:	

NAME _____ *SECTION* _____ *DATE* _____

Arm – Musculature

Front

Outside

Back

Inside

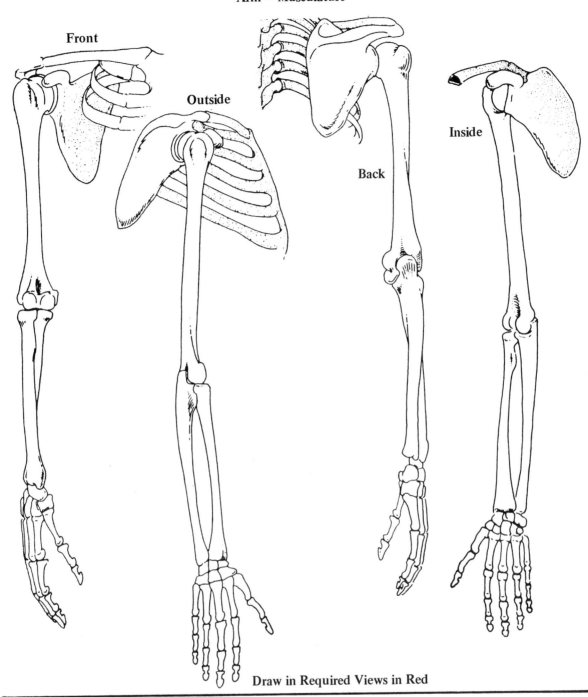

Draw in Required Views in Red

PALMARIS LONGUS

Origin:
Insertion:
Action:

FLEXOR CARPI RADIALIS

Origin:
Insertion:
Action:

NAME_____ SECTION_____ DATE_____

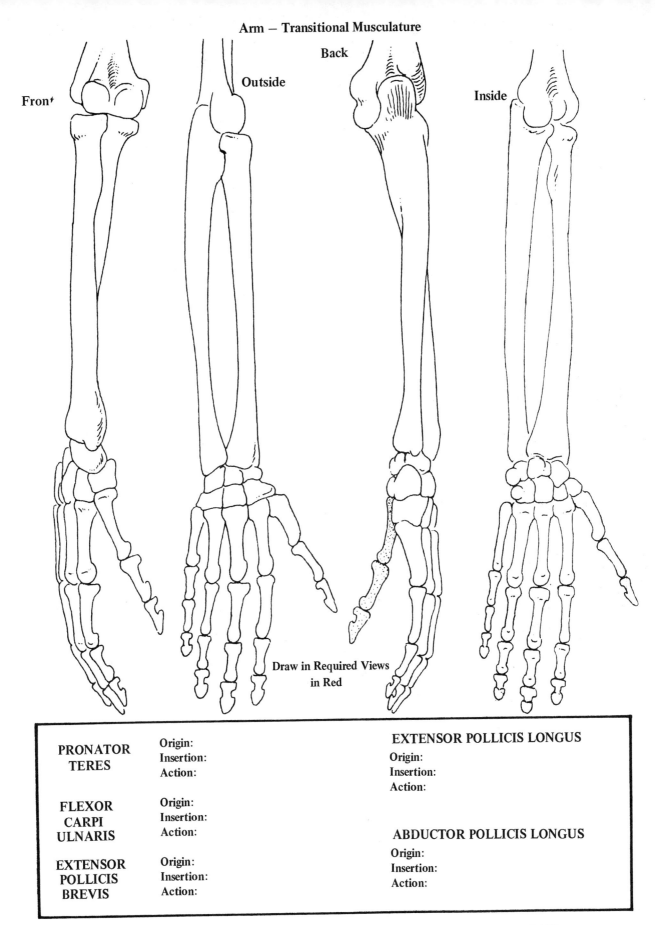

Front

Outside

Back

Inside

Draw in Required Views
in Red

PRONATOR TERES	Origin: Insertion: Action:	EXTENSOR POLLICIS LONGUS Origin: Insertion: Action:
FLEXOR CARPI ULNARIS	Origin: Insertion: Action:	ABDUCTOR POLLICIS LONGUS Origin: Insertion: Action:
EXTENSOR POLLICIS BREVIS	Origin: Insertion: Action:	

*NAME*_____ *SECTION*_____ *DATE*_____

Right — Front View

Fill in muscles of arm in red. Print names of muscles.
Draw horizontal lines in black to muscles

NAME_____ SECTION_____ DATE_____

_____
_____
_____
_____
_____
_____
_____
_____
_____
_____
_____
_____
_____
_____
_____
_____
_____
_____
_____
_____
_____

Right – Outside View

Fill in muscles of arm in red. Print names of muscles.
Draw horizontal lines in black to muscles

Arm – Musculature

_____

_____

_____

_____

_____

_____

_____

_____

_____

_____

_____

_____

_____

_____

_____

_____

_____

_____

_____

Right – Back View

Fill in muscles of arm in red. Print names of muscles.
Draw horizontal lines in black to muscles

NAME_____ SECTION_____ DATE_____

Arm – Musculature

Right – Inside View

_____
_____
_____
_____
_____
_____
_____
_____
_____
_____
_____
_____
_____
_____
_____
_____
_____
_____
_____

Fill in muscles of arm in red. Print names of muscles.
Draw horizontal lines in black to muscles

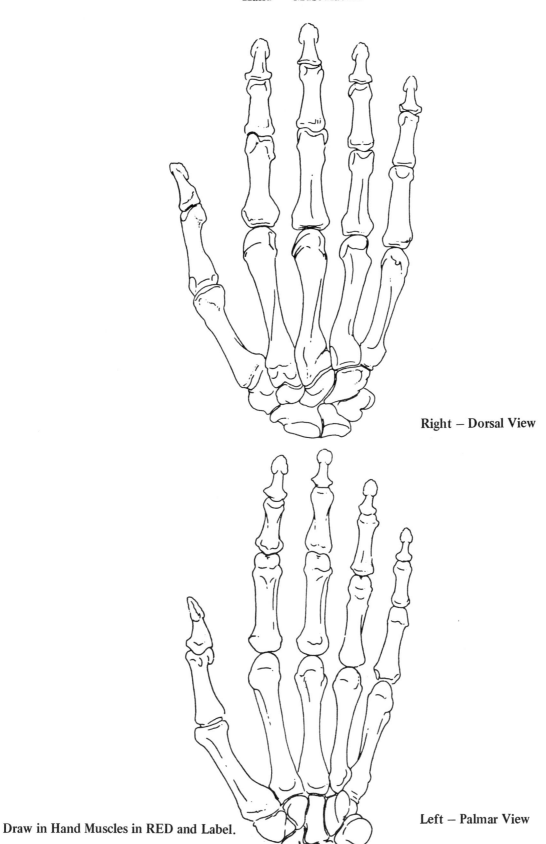

Right — Dorsal View

Left — Palmar View

Draw in Hand Muscles in RED and Label.

NAME_____ SECTION_____, DATE_____

HAND — MUSCULATURE

THUMB GROUP

Name   Action

Abductor Pollicis Brevis
Adductor Pollicis. . . . .
       Oblique Head . . . . ⎤
       Transverse Head . . . . ⎥
Flexor Pollicis Brevis. . . . . ⎦
Opponens Pollicis . . . .

LITTLE FINGER GROUP

Abductor Digiti V . . . .
Flexor Digiti V Brevis . . . .
Opponens Digiti V. . . . .

HAND

Name: **Interossei Dorsales**
Origin: _____
Insertion: _____
Action: _____

Leg – Musculature

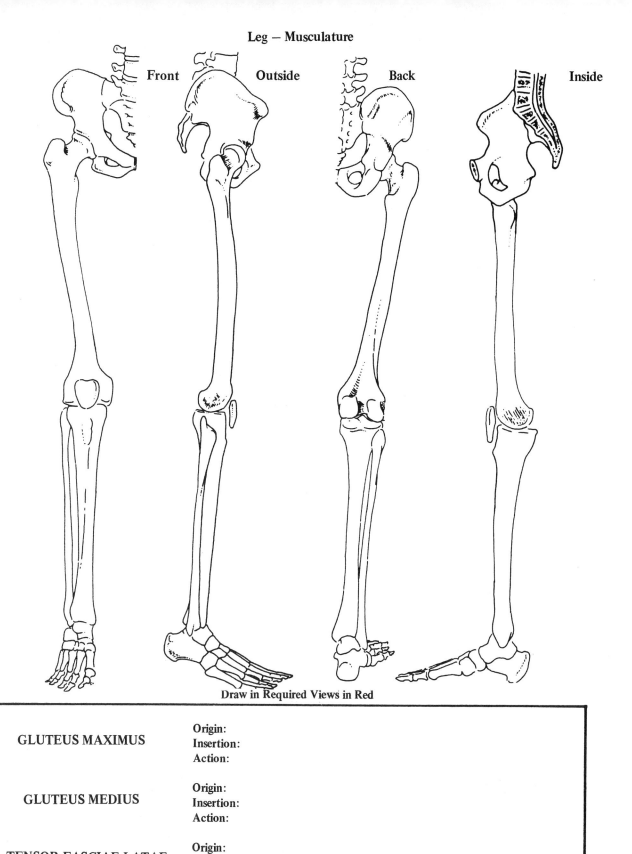

Front   Outside   Back   Inside

Draw in Required Views in Red

GLUTEUS MAXIMUS	**Origin:** **Insertion:** **Action:**	
GLUTEUS MEDIUS	**Origin:** **Insertion:** **Action:**	
TENSOR FASCIAE LATAE	**Origin:** **Insertion:** **Action:**	

*NAME*_____   *SECTION*_____   *DATE*_____

Leg — Musculature

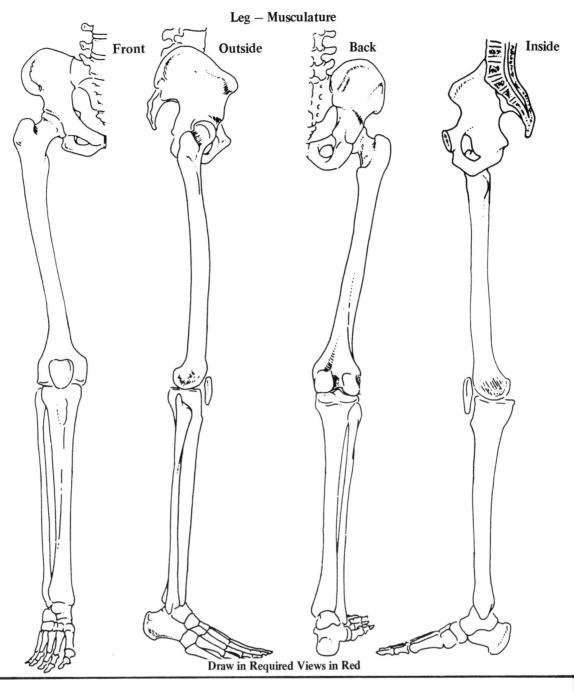

Front   Outside   Back   Inside

Draw in Required Views in Red

A – RECTUS FEMORIS	Origin: Insertion: Action:	
B – VASTUS LATERALIS	Origin: Insertion: Action:	
C – VASTUS MEDIALIS	Origin: Insertion: Action:	

Above are 3 heads of quadriceps to fill in.

NAME_____ SECTION_____ DATE_____

Leg – Musculature

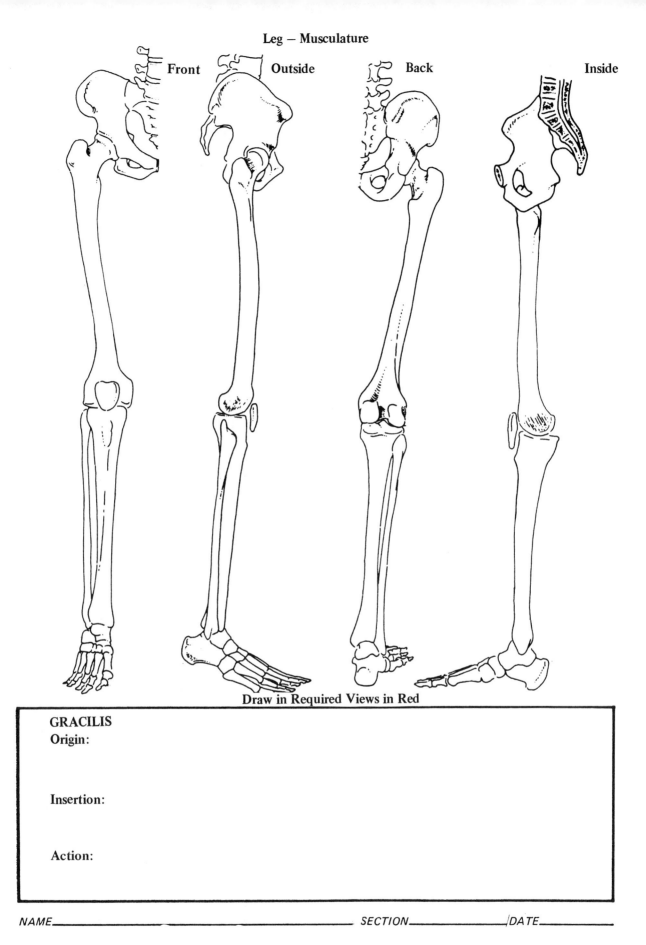

Front   Outside   Back   Inside

Draw in Required Views in Red

GRACILIS
Origin:

Insertion:

Action:

*NAME*_____ _____ *SECTION*_____ */DATE*_____

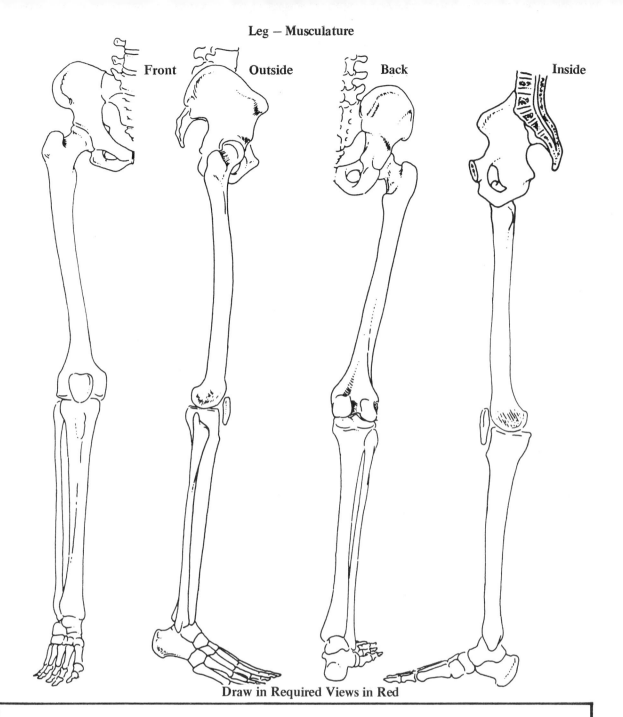

Front   Outside   Back   Inside

Draw in Required Views in Red

PECTINEUS

Origin:
Insertion:
Action:

ADDUCTOR MAGNUS

Origin:
Insertion:
Action:

ADDUCTOR LONGUS

Origin:
Insertion:
Action:

NAME_____ SECTION_____ DATE_____

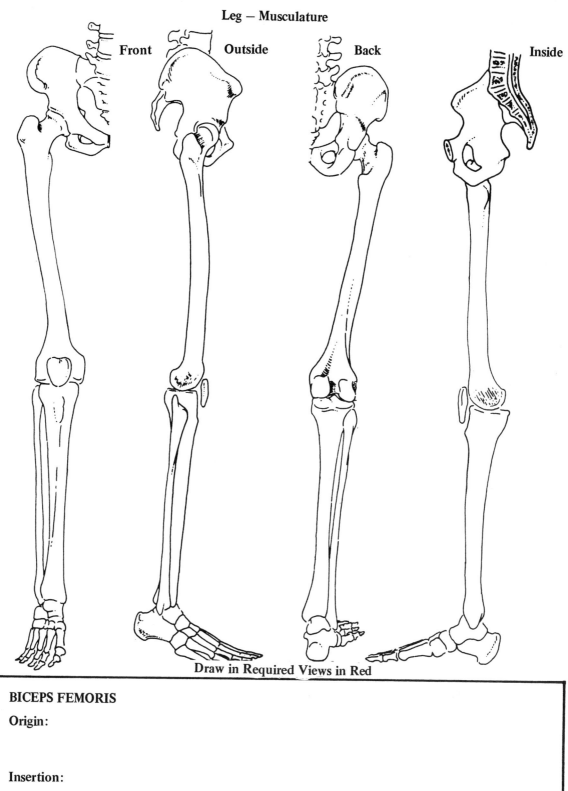

Front   Outside   Back   Inside

Draw in Required Views in Red

BICEPS FEMORIS

Origin:

Insertion:

Action:

Leg – Musculature

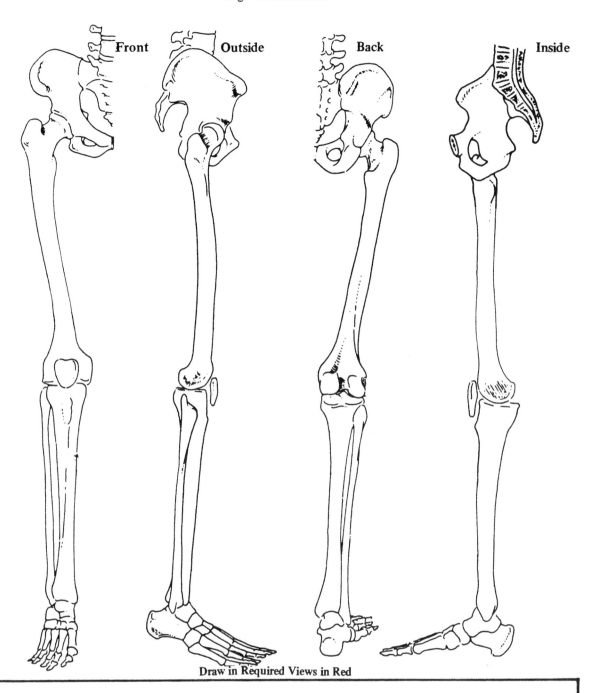

Front   Outside   Back   Inside

Draw in Required Views in Red

SEMITENDINOSUS

Origin:
Insertion:
Action:

SEMIMEMBRANOSUS

Origin:
Insertion:
Action:

NAME_____ SECTION_____ DATE_____

Leg – Musculature

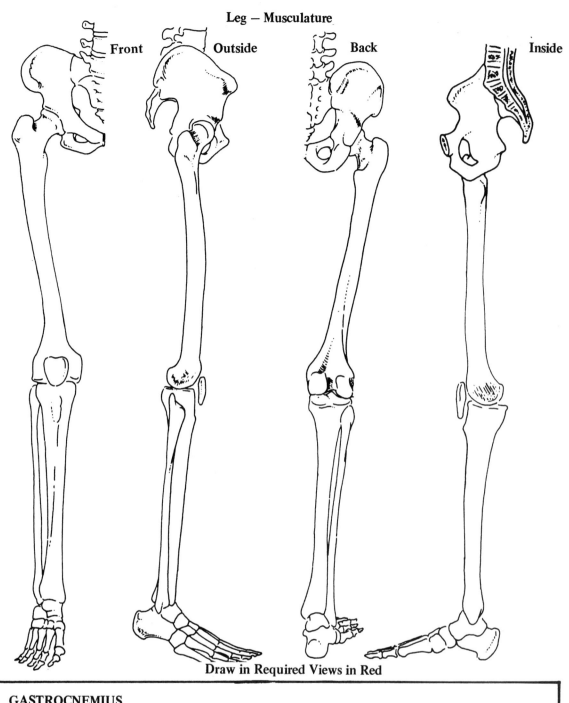

Front　　　Outside　　　Back　　　Inside

Draw in Required Views in Red

GASTROCNEMIUS

Origin:

Insertion:

Action:

Leg – Musculature

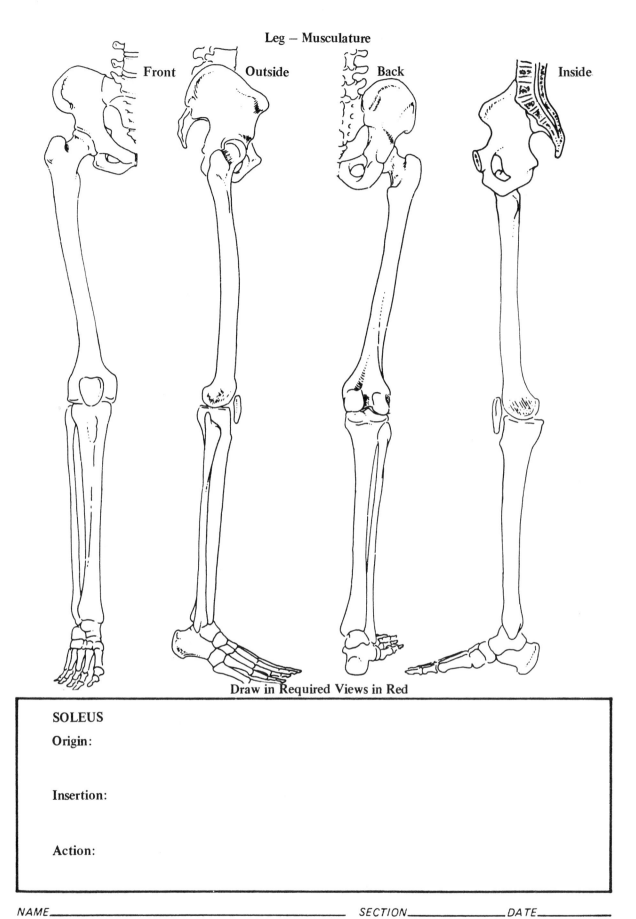

Front   Outside   Back   Inside

Draw in Required Views in Red

SOLEUS

Origin:

Insertion:

Action:

NAME_____   SECTION_____   DATE_____

Leg – Musculature

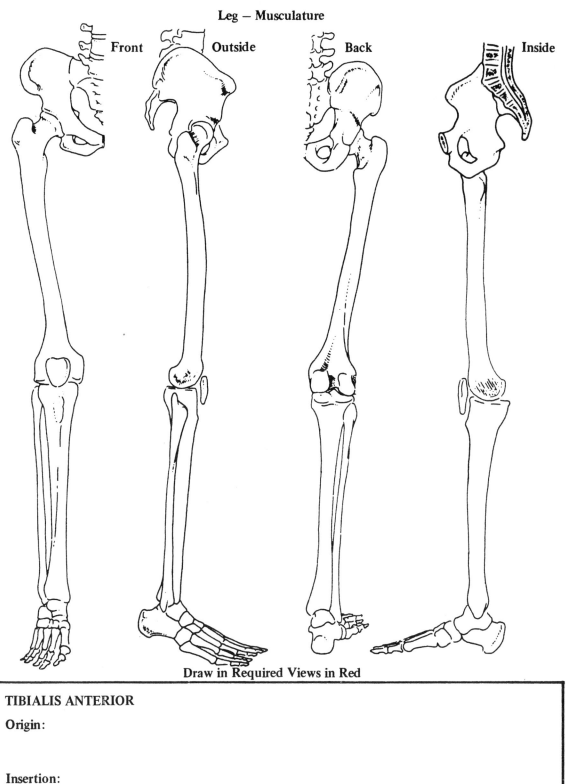

Front   Outside   Back   Inside

Draw in Required Views in Red

TIBIALIS ANTERIOR

Origin:

Insertion:

Action:

Leg – Musculature

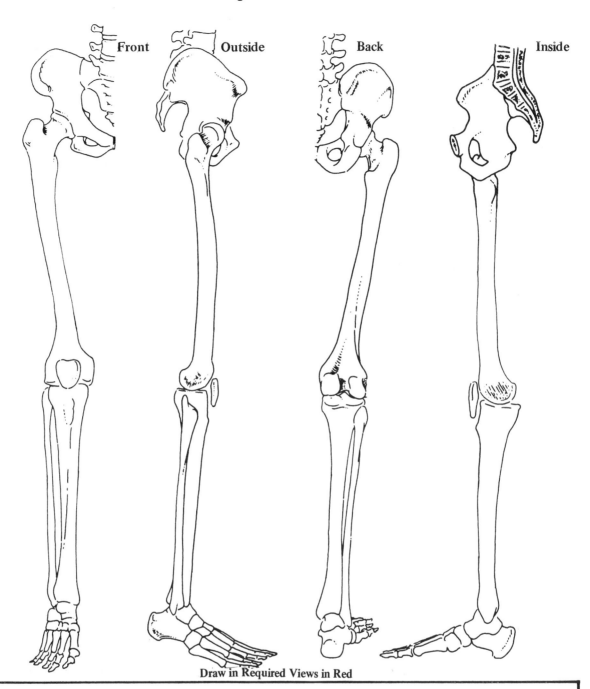

Front Outside Back Inside

Draw in Required Views in Red

EXTENSOR DIGITORUM LONGUS

Origin:
Insertion:
Action:

EXTENSOR HALLUCIS LONGUS

Origin:
Insertion:
Action:

*NAME*_____ *SECTION*_____ *DATE*_____

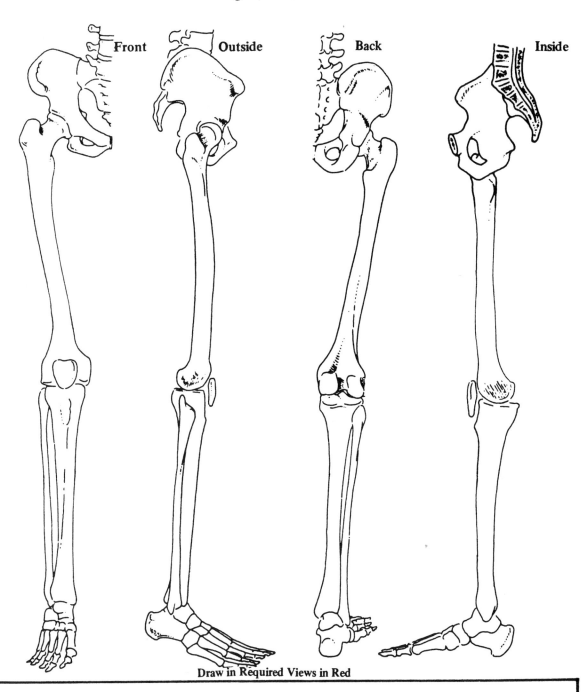

Front   Outside   Back   Inside

Draw in Required Views in Red

PERONEUS LONGUS

Origin:
Insertion:
Action:

PERONEUS BREVIS

Origin:
Insertion:
Action:

NAME _____ *SECTION* _____ *DATE* _____

Leg — Musculature

_____

_____

_____

_____

_____

_____

_____

_____

_____

_____

_____

_____

_____

_____

_____

_____

_____

_____

Right — Front View

Fill in muscles of leg in red. Print names of muscles at left.
Draw horizontal lines in black to muscles.

Right — Side View

Fill in muscles of leg in red. Print names of muscles at left.
Draw horizontal lines in black to muscles.

NAME_____ SECTION_____ DATE_____

Leg — Musculature

_____
_____
_____
_____
_____
_____
_____
_____
_____
_____
_____
_____
_____
_____
_____
_____
_____
_____
_____
_____

Right — Back View

Fill in muscles of leg in red. Print names of muscles at left.
Draw horizontal lines in black to muscles.

NAME_____ SECTION_____ DATE_____

161

Right — Inside View

Fill in muscles of leg in red. Print names of muscles at left.
Draw horizontal lines in black to muscles.

NAME_____ SECTION_____ DATE_____

Foot — Musculature

Right Foot — Dorsal View

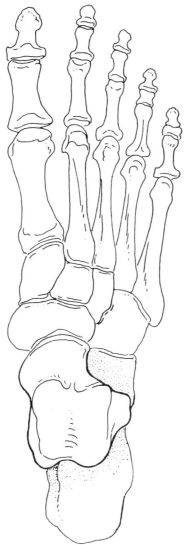

Left Foot — Plantar View

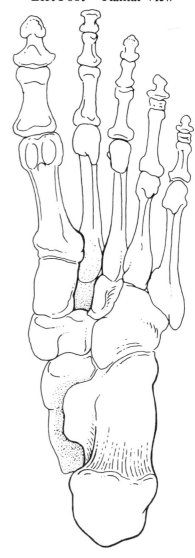

Draw in Required Views in Red

ABDUCTOR DIGITI MINIMI

Origin:
Insertion:
Action:

EXTENSOR DIGITORUM BREVIS

Origin:
Insertion:
Action:

ABDUCTOR HALLUCIS

Origin:
Insertion:
Action:

---

*NAME*_____ *SECTION*_____ *DATE*_____

FOOT – MUSCULATURE

Name   **Abductor Digiti Minimi**

Origin   _____

Insertion   _____

Action   _____

Name   **Abductor Hallucis**

Origin   _____

Insertion   _____

Action   _____

Name   **Extensor Digitorum Brevis**

Origin   _____

Insertion   _____

Action   _____

Fatty Tissue

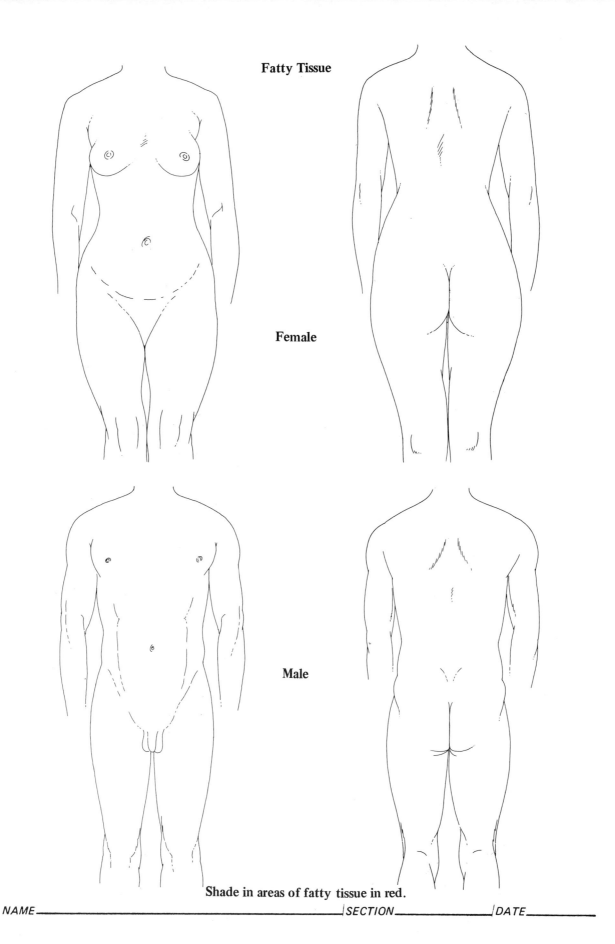

Female

Male

Shade in areas of fatty tissue in red.

Index

CORRESPONDING STUDYBOOK AND WORKBOOK PLATES